The Home Alone Syndrome

A Parent's Handbook for Survival

The Home Alone Syndrome

---

*A Parent's
Handbook
for Survival*

Dr. T. Garrott Benjamin, Jr.

Heaven on Earth Publishing House
Indianapolis, Indiana

The Home Alone Syndrome
Copyright © 1994 by Dr. T. Garrott Benjamin, Jr.
Light of the World Christian Church
5640 E. 38th Street
Indianapolis, Indiana 46218

Printed in the United States of America

All Scripture in King James Version.

Library of Congress Cataloging in Publication Data
Benjamin, Jr., T. Garrott
     The Home Alone Syndrome

1. Family   2. Motivation   3. Religious
     I. Title

93-079926
     CIP

ISBN 0-9637171-2-X

CONTENTS

ACKNOWLEDGMENTS

Once again, I am presenting an expanded manuscript that began as a sermon. Pastors and preachers are some of our nation's most sensitive and thoughtful communicators of divine truth. Each week they write another chapter often for only their file drawer to see. This practice must come to an end. I want to be an encourager to all pastors and teachers: WRITE ON! You will do just fine once you get over the fact that your primary audience is not the professor but the parent or the person in the pew...the one on the street or in the suite. That is the perspective I put to work in my preaching as well as my writing a practical perspective on the perplexing problems of ordinary people is my approach. I hope you like this book and I hope it makes you a better parent or prospective parent.

I owe a deep debt of gratitude to the members of my beloved congregation for their unconditional love and support that has allowed me time away from them to write this little book with the big message. I have also been blessed with an unusually efficient and effervescent secretary, Pam Dixon, who typed and retyped manuscripts over and over again *without complaint or criticism.* I also want to thank Billye Bridges and Alice Hord for their precise proofreading and their sensible suggestions. To my friend and editorial assistant, Robert C. Larson, I am also most grateful. Last but not least, I want to thank my Queen, Beverly, who has been a faithful wife, friend and confidant for over 26 years. My three sons have been blessed by a mother who made it her business not to leave them *home alone.*

But most of all I want to thank Almighty God who gives me the strength to climb higher mountains on my way home. *What a mighty God we serve. Angels bow before Him. Heaven and Earth adore Him. What a mighty God we serve!*

Peace,
T. Garrott Benjamin, Jr.
Light of the World Christian Church
Indianapolis, Indiana

ABOUT THE AUTHOR

T. Garrott Benjamin, Jr., is a native of St. Louis, Missouri and was raised in Cleveland, Ohio by a single parent grandmother. Since 1969, he has been Senior Pastor of the historic 3,000 member *Light of the World Christian Church* (est. 1866) in Indianapolis, Indiana.

Dr. Benjamin is both an innovator and a motivator. His burden for young people birthed the first *Respect Academy* for children in the nation, and his burden for souls birthed the *Heaven on Earth* television ministry, and now, the *Heaven on Earth Publishing House* which published the best seller *Boys to Men.*

His ministry has been featured in the *Congressional Record, Washington Post, Jet Magazine, The Disciple Magazine,* and other national periodicals. He has written numerous articles and sermons that have been published in a wide variety of periodicals and books.

Dr. Benjamin's ministry has also been seen and felt throughout the world through national cable television (TBN, BET and LeSea) and the Armed Forces Television Network. Dr. Benjamin and Light of the World were featured by ABC in the national telecast called "The Soul of Christmas." The British Broadcasting Company (BBC) featured Dr. Benjamin and Light of the World in a religious documentary called *The Long Search* which was seen throughout the free world. He has preached on almost every continent, and has recently returned from speaking engagements and fact-finding tours of Australia, Cuba and Russia. He continues to be a highly sought after preacher and lecturer. He is as comfortable in the pulpit as he is in the classroom. He has the uncanny ability to "walk with kings, and yet not lose the common touch" when it comes to communicating God's Word.

He is host producer of the longest running public affairs television program in Indianapolis, "Livin' for the City." Dr. Benjamin is a graduate of St. Louis University, in St. Louis, Missouri, and Christian Theological Seminary in Indianapolis, Indiana where he earned the Master of Divinity and the Doctor of Ministry degrees. He also holds several honorary doctorates, the most recent coming from Christian Theological Seminary. He is married to his beautiful helpmate, Beverly, and has three fine sons.

FOREWARD

The movies "Home Alone" and "Home Alone II" were family oriented comedies about a young child who was accidentally left to fend for himself. While both movies were hilarious, the fact is that in real life being home alone for most children is not funny, but tragic and often destructive.

The Home Alone Syndrome by Dr. T. Garrott Benjamin, Jr., lays out for us the problems that face an entire generation and nation when children are home alone. Dr. Benjamin, however, takes us beyond the problems to empowering solutions that can transform potential gangsters and children at risk into members of G.A.N.G. (God's Anointed New Generation).

Dr. Benjamin's *The Home Alone Syndrome* is written for parents, children, teachers, preachers, social workers, lawyers and all people who are concerned about redeeming what many are calling a "lost" generation. As Dr. Benjamin so succinctly states, "This is not a lost generation but a left generation." This book equips us with the necessary skills to reach a generation of victims and move them toward victory. Read it, live it!

Buy some books and pass them on to your friends. *The Home Alone Syndrome* is a must reading for all those who will accept the challenge to liberate the lost and set the captives free.

Dr. Frank M. Reid, III, Pastor

Bethel AME Church

Baltimore, MD

I dedicate this book to my sainted grandmother,
Mrs. Marilla Jackson,
who made it her business never
to let me come home to an empty house
or an empty heart. Thanks, Mama.
Keep the light in the window.

TGB

PROLOGUE

T o say America's children are at risk is the understatement of the decade. Broken homes are robbing millions of our best and our brightest from at least one full-time parent. An escalation in the number of women in the workplace, compounded by an insidious materialism and workaholism have put our children either in the care of others, or left them home alone. American parents should be shutting off the TV and turning on the basics of honest communication with their children.

Why are we so slow in recognizing that parents need to be home with their children? Why are so many parents casting their flesh-and-blood treasures upon the rocks and shoals of an angry sea to put their faith in what they *really* love and trust — money, material objects, status and their own selfish desires? Edward Zigler, a professor of child development at Yale University, a scholar who has spent his professional career fighting the abuses of child care says, "We are cannibalizing children. Children are dying in this system, never mind achieving optimum development."

In *The Home Alone Syndrome*, I have done my best to address some of the issues that are destroying the boys and girls in these later years of the 20th century. I have already written briefly about the *home alone* phenomenon in my first book *Boys to Men*. But *The Home Alone Syndrome* is a longer, more thorough treatment of this chilling subject. I am going to tell it like it really is. This is a subject we must either deal with creatively and honestly or live to regret the day we thought we could treat our children as so many expendables in our personal quest for personal fulfillment.

I write this book for all my brothers and sisters — not out of joy, but from the heavy heart of a pastor who daily sees the consequences of the *home alone syndrome*. These words are for you parents who do not have to leave your children home alone, but you do it because you *think* your absence will not matter in the long run. I trust this book shows you how terribly wrong you are. I also write for you single parents who are frustrated, angry and confused about *having* to leave your children home alone *when you do not want to!* You, too, are looking for answers.

My heart goes out especially for those precious black boys and girls who, right now, are left *home alone*. Daily, they come home from school to be greeted not by the loving arms of a mother, but instead by the bizarre, offbeat offerings of baby-sitters who host the TV tabloids and talk shows.

Am I angry? You better believe I am angry. Rage would be a much better word — a righteous indignation that will not let me go. I do pray, however, that I will see substantive results *before* Jesus comes. I promise you my anger will not abate until *"together we marshal our best efforts to identify the problem, produce intelligent, workable solutions, and then work those solutions."* I have no desire to be a lone voice crying in the wilderness. But if necessary that is where I am willing to start. This is a together-we-must-do-it effort and not a one-man show!

I have prayed for months that God would give me the right words to communicate what I have to say in this book. During that time I have also prayed for you, the reader, that God would enlighten your heart, expand your mind and free your spirit to give you an openness to accepting this vital message for our day. Much of what you read in this book may be hard to swallow. But this is no time to pull punches. This is not the hour to wade timidly into the shallow waters where we pretend things are just fine! My brother and sister, things are *not* just fine. The waves are high and our ships are in danger of sinking. We must not stand idly by shouting encouragement to our children from the shore. Our boys and girls need life rafts and life preservers, but mostly they need stay-at-home parents who are willing to get into the water with them and rescue them before it is too late. We must act and *we must act now.* Tomorrow is too late. I hurt for our children and I hurt bad.

- I hurt for children who are left *home alone.*
- I hurt for children whose closest companion is the telephone.
- I hurt for little black boys and girls who think that daycare is the best care they can receive.
- I hurt for little black boys and girls who call the baby-sitter "mamma" and the pizza delivery man "daddy."
- I hurt for children whose primary exercise is working the remote control and whose primary teacher is the television.
- I hurt for children who must decide each day whether they will treat their house as a hotel or as a haven.

You and I may already be good friends. But whether we have made each other's acquaintance or not, I want you to know that God loves you and your children and so do I. For their sake — and for the sake of the race — *please* never again leave them *home alone.*

Peace after Justice,
TGB
April 1994
Indianapolis

"When the television set becomes
the primary substitute for interpersonal
communication, that is a sin;
when the talk show hosts become
the substitute stand-in, stand-up parents
for our children, that is a sin."

TGB

* * *

Proverbs 29:15 says,
"The rod and reproof give wisdom: but a child left to
himself bringeth his mother to shame."

* * *

"Our children are not a lost generation
but a *left* generation."

TGB

1

THE HOME ALONE *SIN*DROME

F amily life in America has changed — generally for the worse. The home was once nuclear, comprised of a father who worked, and a mother who took care of the children and helped make the home a happy place for all. My how the once honored word *homemaker* has fallen on hard times, and how the word *homewrecker* has strangely become a more palatable substitute. What was once *nuclear* has now become *unclear.* Parents and children all seem to suffer from *role confusion,* each doing his or her own thing, with any semblance of discipline and personal responsibility fast going the way of the dinosaur. The African proverb is true to a fault: *A single bracelet does not jingle.* It takes more than one person to make a sound, to make a home, and to make a difference. That goes for any relationship worthy of the name. Sadly, children who are left *home alone* are placed in the greatest jeopardy of all.

America's Children at Risk

The dictionary defines a syndrome as a *group of symptoms that together are characteristic of a specific condition, or disease; a pattern of symptoms that indicate a particular social condition.* This definition gives us the clinical information we need to understand a medical or social phenomenon, but it does *not* make a value judgment on whatever those conditions might be. That's why I have created a new word, *sin*drome, which when used in this chapter, will remind you that when a child is left home alone it must be regarded as a sin; when the television set becomes the substitute for interpersonal communication, that is a sin, and sin is *anything* or *anyone* that separates you from God. Sadly, there are numerous disorders and diseases prominent in today's society, many with disastrous effects on our children.

"AIDS is killing our boys and girls, adolescents and young adults in record numbers. AIDS is now being touted as the greatest killer of young adult males between the ages of 25 and 44. However, as sobering as these statistics might be, there is an even more debilitating disease which is overwhelming our culture. It is the *Home Alone Sindrome.*"

TGB

AIDS is killing our boys and girls, adolescents and young adults in record numbers. It is now being touted as the greatest killer of young adult males between the ages of 25 and 44. However, as sobering as these statistics might be, there is an even more debilitating disease which is overwhelming our culture. It is the *Home Alone Sindrome.*

America's blood stream has been polluted and infected with what some have called a terminal "dis-ease." Our children are being left alone without supervision or continued parental support. When a child is left alone, eventually a nation of children is left alone, leaving the entire country at risk. AIDS may kill the body, but the *Home Alone Sindrome* kills the soul.

> "The tragic truth is that America has become a key player in this insidious, international conspiracy against children, and it has started in our homes. We are leaving our children home alone, and we are paying the price for our sindrome. Proverbs 29:15 says, 'The rod and reproof give wisdom: but a child left to himself bringeth his mother to shame.'"
>
> TGB

Most of us are aware of the appalling statistics of children at risk in other nations. In Brazil more than 4,600 street children have been killed in the last 36 months. An estimated 40 million abandoned children live on the streets of urban Latin America. Innocent boys and girls are part of a growing *sex for hire* slavery now sweeping Europe, Afrika, Asia and the countries of Central and South America. This *sin*drome is feeding the sexual sadism and prurient purposes of emotionally sick men and women throughout the world.

The tragic truth is that America has become a key player in this insidious, international conspiracy against children, and it has started in our homes. We are leaving our children home alone, and we are paying the price for our *sin*drome. Proverbs 29:15 says, "The rod and reproof give wisdom: but a child left to himself bringeth his mother to shame." I hope you believe what the Word says, but more important, I hope you know, and believe in your heart, that the Word *works!* God's Word is sure, but we must be sure to obey it. When we do not court the Word, we wind up courting chaos and dancing with disaster.

Today, we have a generation of disobedient children who are the sons and daughters of disobedient parents. So let us get one thing straight at the outset: we must stop blaming the victims — our children — and begin educating the parents. If a taxi runs a red light and kills a child, we must not blame the child for crossing the street correctly. The blame must be placed on the driver of the taxi for being out of control. When a child is left home alone, it is not the fault of the child. It is the parents who must answer for the errors of their ways.

We desperately need to address this dis-ease with a fervent search for a cure. We need to call this sin the *sin*drome it is. We must humble ourselves, repent and ask God for forgiveness. Repentance is not simply saying, *I'm sorry,* however. Repentance is *doing something about the problem.* It is first confessing it and then addressing it. It is more than verbal acknowledgment. It is turning our backs on the sin itself.

The *Home Alone Sindrome* is a vicious cycle of the abandonment of children by parents. It is not just a mistake. It is not just a problem. It is sin! This sin can only be dealt with through repentance and the cleansing power of a redeeming Christ. We still sing, "What can wash away my sin? What can make me clean within? Nothing but the blood of Jesus." There is no easy way out. The cure for the *Home Alone Sindrome* takes work, effort, and major surgery of heart and mind.

It requires a paradigm shift of enormous proportions, a shift that will come about with a conscious renewal of our commitment to children. It need not be a return to the alleged romanticism of yesteryear, but it must be a fast forward to the best that is within us.

The Black Child's Dilemma

Slavery, segregation, discrimination and racism all have a peculiar effect upon the black child's dilemma. The problem is bad enough when we talk about the situation "in general," but it is

"The Home Alone Sindrome is a vicious cycle
of the abandonment of children by parents.
It is not just a mistake. It is not just a problem.
It is sin! This sin can only be dealt with through
repentance and the cleansing power of a
redeeming Christ. There is no easy way out.
The cure for the *Home Alone Sindrome* takes
work, effort, and major surgery of heart and mind."

TGB

almost unbearable when we refer to its impact on Afrikan Americans specifically. If it is bad for children, it is many times worse for our young black brothers and sisters, because society still operates on the basis of color and race.

A black child is the product of the black woman and the black man who must deal with the pressure and pain of bigotry and white racism on a daily basis. This inordinate pressure has contributed to the breakdown of the black family and the growing incidence of the *Home Alone Sindrome.* You cannot start people 100 yards behind in a 440 race and assume that everyone will finish at the same time. The black child is the child of the oppressed. The black child is the child of a society where there are practically no black CEO's in the top 500 companies in America. A black child is the child of a culture where there are no black owners of National Football League teams, or National Baseball teams, or National Basketball teams. At the 1994 NBA All Star Game, most of the game was played with all black teams but yet virtually every owner in the league is white. We are the entertainers but not the entrepreneurs. The 1994 Academy Awards had three black nominees, yet we buy more than 50% of all theater tickets. I appreciate the message and talent of those who produced *Schindler's List* but when are we going to get on that ever shrinking list that allows us entrance to the American mainstream? And on the retail front, today almost every major shopping center in America is devoid of black ownership. What's up? Where is our race? Where are our business leaders when we need leading the most?

I read an article in the paper recently that riveted my attention on what has become a tragedy in so many black families. This sister admitted when she felt depressed or unloved she just had another baby. Her loneliness and poverty of spirit ultimately produced three sons. She said when her boys were infants, she cuddled them; when they were toddlers, she slapped them, and when they grew to be little boys she punished them for all the times she had been wronged by the *other* men in her life.

What a tragedy! We all know this is not a black issue alone. But this story describes the challenges being faced in black households all across this nation. From the cuddling, to the slapping, to the punishing, it is often just one more short step for a black sister to become so frustrated that she simply walks out whenever she pleases, leaving her children home alone.

"A black child is the product of the black woman and the black man who must deal with the pressure and pain of bigotry and white racism on a daily basis. This inordinate pressure has contributed to the breakdown of the black family, and the growing incidence of the *Home Alone Sindrome.* You cannot start people 100 yards behind in a 440 race and assume that everyone is going to finish at the same time.

TGB

This is the dilemma. When you subtract significant others from the *black family,* you always leave the child vulnerable and unable to care for himself. Let us be honest, realistic and responsible: a child is not an adult. A child must crawl before he can walk and walk before he can run. Maturity has not yet come. The child cannot make his or her own decisions, and thus the dilemma is magnified. The child is caught in between. Yes, the child needs to be more mature, but that is an unrealistic expectation to place on any boy or girl. Maturity is hastened, however, when there is a *caring someone* at home — like a father and a mother — to help that little one through the increasingly difficult process of growing up. As I said in *Boys to Men,* it takes time to make the transition, it can never happen overnight. *And no child can do it all alone.*

When black boys and girls find themselves in harm's way,

they have few tools by which to defend themselves. Even if they had them, many would not know how to use them. It reminds me of the story of the wildebeest, an Afrikan buffalo-like animal, which seems to be in a constant state of childlike immaturity, but in its history has somehow learned the principles of survival. Alone, the wildebeest is vulnerable to the attack of any predator, most likely the lion or the leopard. But when it is surrounded by a host of other wildebeests, it moves with great security and strength. It survives because it:

- Stays with the pack
- Stays on track
- Never looks back, and just
- Keeps on running

These principles of survival learned from the wildebeest will help anyone who must survive in the wild of today's society. Right now, since we are telling it like it is in this book, Afrikan American families have become part of that wild, uncontrolled environment. That's why we need to stick together and protect our young from a social situation that is becoming increasingly vicious. Now is the time for black families everywhere to sing with voices strong and clear the great hymn of the faith, *"Come home, come home. Ye who are weary, come home. Earnestly, tenderly, Jesus is calling, calling O sinner, come home."*

Momma and Daddy...come home to your children now. Do not leave them to their own devices. Keep them from trading

> "Momma and Daddy...come home to your children now. Do not leave them to their own devices. Keep them from trading handguns instead of baseball cards. Help them get out of the neighborhood gang and into the Jesus gang. Parents, help your children become responsible by becoming responsible yourselves."
>
> TGB

handguns instead of baseball cards. Help them get out of the neighborhood gang and into the Jesus gang. Help your children become *responsible by becoming responsible yourselves.* As I wrote in my book, *Boys to Men,* "We can no longer afford to match black boys with boomboxes against white boys with computers. Remember the words of the Apostle Paul... "When I was a child, I acted like a child, understood like a child, but when I became a man — when I became responsible — I threw away childish things" (I Corinthians 13:11, paraphrased).

"If we are going to teach our little boys and girls how to become men and women, there must be a nationwide effort, starting in our homes and in our churches, to help the potential man and woman *inside the little child* to stand up to be counted, to be responsible, and to become the real men and women God wants them to be. It won't happen overnight but it is not supposed to happen overnight. *We are going to have to go through it to get to it!"*

Ain't Nobody Home

I never remember coming home to an empty house as a child. The saintly, God-fearing, single-parent grandmother who raised me was always there. Whatever she was doing, she stopped doing it to be there for *me* when I got home. She made arrangements for *me*. She inconvenienced herself for *me*. She made herself uncomfortable for *me*. She sacrificed for *me*. She did all this because she loved *me*. She knew even back then there were influences that were negative, and she determined to protect *me*. Sometimes I wished she would not have been quite so good about her *always being there* but there she was, sure as night follows day. The Apostle Paul said in Philippians 2:4,5,7 and 8,

> "Look not every man on his own things, but every man also on the things of others. Let this mind be in you, which was also in Christ Jesus: But made himself of no reputation, and took upon him the form of a servant, and was made in the likeness of men: And being found in fashion as a man, he humbled himself, and became obedient unto death, even the death of the cross."

If on any occasion my grandmother could not find me, she

would put to use her internal, God-given P.A. system to rectify that problem. Here's how it worked. We lived in the middle of the block, at 10532 Bryant Avenue, in Cleveland, Ohio. My grandmother could simply turn to the right or to the left of our porch, fill her lungs with air and yell T-O-M-M-Y. I knew I could stall Grandma for about three yells, but then I figured I had better have my feet planted on the front lawn or my bottom would know it for hours to come.

You see, I was never left *home alone.* I was never victimized by parental neglect, societal neglect or educational neglect. My grandmother did not enjoy the advantage of having a husband who would be protector, provider and priest for our home, but that did not stop her from fulfilling her responsibilities to me. She believed the verse in Proverbs that says… "A child left to himself bringeth his mother to shame." She made sure there were adult males in my life. Sam took me swimming. Mr. Caldwell took me fishing. Turner taught me how to work in the yard and Frank was the older brother I never had. So just because you are a single parent *that does not mean your child should be without a mentor.* This is particularly true for boys, because mothers have a tendency *to raise their daughters and love their sons.* If we look hard enough, we usually can find a qualified mentor: an uncle, cousin or friend. But of course, the preferable mentor would be *the father* of the child.

No Thanks, Talk Show Hosts!

How things have changed. It is not necessary to read too many

> "It is one thing to be an orphan in a home
> for orphans; it is another thing
> to be an orphan in your *own* home."
>
> TGB

headlines or watch that many CNN reports to realize we are paying the price for the abandonment of our children. Drug use among our children is on the increase. Their preoccupation with guns and gangs is driving our law enforcement agencies to distraction. Teenage pregnancies are out of sight. AIDS is killing our young and threatens to annihilate a whole generation. Lack of respect for parents is so widespread that the word *standards* is no longer in the vocabulary of most children. History is repeating itself. Even the Apostle Paul reflected on his contemporary culture in II Timothy 3:1-11. The first three verses of that passage read…

> *This know also, that in the last days perilous times shall come. For men shall be lovers of their own selves, covetous, boasters, proud, blasphemers, disobedient to parents, unthankful, unholy, without natural affection, truce-breakers, false accusers, incontinent, fierce, despisers of those that are good…*

If these verses are not as fresh as today's headlines then I don't know what kinds of books and magazines you are reading these days. (I encourage you to take some time and read what else Paul had to say in this chapter of counsel to Timothy, his young son in the faith.)

It is one thing to be an orphan in a home for orphans; it is another thing to be an orphan in your *own* home. So who takes care of your children when there is nobody home? One convenient solution is to let the peep show hosts of morning and afternoon television raise the children. Let the kids learn about life from people who live and breathe the world of the bizarre.

For the past several months, I have been making notes on the content of just a few of the 17 or more so-called TV *talk shows* now puking their perversion and promiscuity into America's homes. For your *de-edification,* here are some of the subjects our children have been exposed to in the last few days on programs that pander to perversion and putrefaction.

* Harmonious divorces

* Pampered dogs

* Stalking victims

* Women afraid of men they sent to jail

* Men who killed their wives' lovers

* Women who harm their children for attention

* Parents ashamed of their children

* Female porn stars

  * Playboy-posing family

    * Serial killers

      * Child-killing husbands

* Sexually precocious teens

  * Teenage girls compete for sex

    * Woman says husband forced her to kill

      * Abusive boyfriends

* Winning back cheating husbands

  * College student who shot her pimp

    * Moms allowing teens to have sex at home

      * Women who have sex just to get pregnant

* Crack addicts who sold their babies

  * Man with seven wives

    * Teenage transsexuals await the operation

      * Psychic healers

* Exhibitionist spouses

  * Women in love with criminals…

and the list of the banal and the bizarre goes on! These shows, produced in the sordid shallow sewers of what was once a reasonably responsible media are sending diabolical messages to our children. These programs are taking the place of parental priorities and principles. But if you think the subjects of these daily televised *peep shows* are disgraceful, then take a look at the lecherous lyrics from the popular songs your children are probably listening to. One song, recorded in 1993, is called *Freak Me,* by Silk...

Freak me baby - ah yeah
Freak me baby - ah yeah . . just like that
Freak me baby - ah yeah
Freak me baby - ah yeah

Chorus
Let me lick you up and down
Till you say stop.
Let me play with your body baby
Make you real hot!
Let me do all the things
You want me to do
'Cause tonight baby,
I want to get freaky with you.

Baby don't you understand
I wanna be your next man.
I wanna make your body scream
Then you'll know just what I mean.
(You know what I mean)
Twenty-four karat gold
I wanna lick you up and down
And then I wanna lay down and come
Oh, so slow!

I love the taste of whip cream - hey
Spread it on and don't be mean

You know I can't resist you girl
I'll fly you all around the world
(All around the world)
I wanna see your body drip
Come on, let me take a sip
(Come on, Come on, Come on, Come on)
So call what you cherish most
'Cause when I brag, I like to brag and boast.

"My message to parents? Get in control.
Turn off the TV. Regulate the music. Do you really
want your child to hear songs like this...
or see an estimated 40,000 murders
on television before he or she is 18?
A judge in Indianapolis told me recently that
there has been a 73% increase in sex crimes
among teenagers within the past 12 months!"

TGB

This is what children are listening to. You be the judge. Since this song was released, the rap music industry has taken crude, raw and vulgar to a new level. My message to parents? Get in control. Turn off the T.V. Regulate the music. Do you really want your child to hear songs like this...or see an estimated 40,000 murders on television before he or she is 18?

A judge here in Indianapolis told me recently that there has

> "And when you say NO, remind them that
> the word NO is a complete sentence."
>
> TGB

been a 73% increase in sex crimes among teenagers within the past 12 months! Yes, there are a lot of reasons for these statistics, but a key factor is an unbridled acceptance of the media as the perpetual baby-sitter for our children who are left *home alone.* This dis-ease must stop. Parents, let your children know you will not tolerate this filth. And when you say NO, remind them that the word NO is a complete sentence. Yes, it is going to take work and eternal vigilance. It will be difficult, and your children may fight you every inch of the way. No one said it would be easy. Just remember that the word *easy* appears only once in the New Testament, and then in connection with a yoke. It is quite possible to work without results. But there will never be results without work.

Weeds grow all by themselves; flowers demand cultivation.

> "No one said it would be easy. Just remember
> that the word *easy* appears only once in the
> New Testament, and then in connection with a
> yoke. It is quite possible to work without results.
> But there will never be results without work."
>
> TGB

And the flowers who are our children cannot grow properly if they are left home alone. That is why parents must take the lead in working *for* their children and not *against* them. I encourage you to exchange phone numbers with your child's teachers. Go to the school to discuss their grades at the end of each grading period. Is this work on your behalf? Yes it is. But let's get back to some self-denial. So you are a little inconvenienced. So what? You are the parent and it is your responsibility to be a little inconvenienced. We've come through the *me decade* and it is now time for a *century* of sacrifice and service.

Jesus tells us to take up our cross, because if there is no cross there will definitely be no crown. This kind of teaching goes against everything you and I hear and see. It flies in the face of all

---

"Exchange phone numbers with your child's teachers. Go to the school to discuss their grades at the end of each grading period.
Is this work on your behalf? Yes it is. But let's get back to some self-denial. So you are a little inconvenienced. So what? You are the parent and it is your responsibility to be a little inconvenienced. We've come through the *me decade* and it is now time for a century of sacrifice and service."

TGB

our advertising and the manipulative ploys of money-hungry media moguls. But if we are to save this generation of children, we had better be prepared to think *God's* thoughts and not the thoughts of a sensual, selfish, dollar-dazed society. It is not enough just to make a *good living;* you must make a *good life* for you *and* your children. *What does it profit a man if he should gain the whole world and lose his own soul?* What good is a house if it is not a home? What good is a job if there is no joy? What is the value in being involved in everything in the community and lose your children?

"What good is a job if there is no joy? What is the value in being involved in everything in the community and lose your children?"

TGB

Left, Not Lost

"I'll rob you in Compton and blast you in Miami..."
From Dre Day,
By Dr. Dre and Snoop Doggy Dog

This generation of children is not so much *lost* as it is *left.* Not so much ornery as orphaned. Not so much niggardly as neglected. It is not so much that our children have become irresponsible as it is that vast numbers of parents have become irrelevant. It is not so much a question of juvenile delinquency as it is parental delinquency. My brothers and sisters, our children are not lost, they have just been left *home alone* to fend for themselves. We have forced them to figure it out for themselves. Up until now. Now is the time to reverse the sins of the past and provide our children with the future they deserve.

We are paying a tremendous price for this nationwide abandonment of children within their own homes. Ask any parent, teacher, or principal. Ask the police who cuff our children, the reporter who writes the stories, the camera person who records the images of violence for an entire nation to see. Oh yes, they know all about *home alone*. They know some married couples are doing their *worst* and that some single parents are doing their *best*. But the end result is the same: children are left *home alone*.

While most children of single parents somehow seem to make

> "This generation of children is not so much *lost* as it is *left*. Not so much ornery, as it is orphaned. Not so much niggardly as neglected. It is not so much that our children have become irresponsible as it is that vast numbers of parents have become irrelevant. It is not so much a question of juvenile delinquency as it is parental delinquency."
>
> TGB

it despite the odds, there are still troubling signs on the horizon. Twenty-seven per cent of U.S. babies today are born out of wedlock. *That is a five-fold increase over the past three decades.* One in every five children in America is born into poverty. Boys and girls of never-married mothers are six times more likely to be poor than those living with two parents. Perhaps an even more chilling fact is that children in 45 percent of *newly formed* families are now considered *at risk* because the mother is a teenager, unmarried, undereducated, or all three. And when you go out on three strikes you don't know *how* to take care of a baby because you are a baby yourself. How easy it is then to leave those precious babies home alone. Consider these terrifying statistics from 1994 and consider the horrifying realities of the years to come:

- Every 92 seconds a black baby is born into poverty.
- Every 42 minutes a black baby dies.
- Every 3 minutes a black baby is born to a teen mother.
- Every 3 minutes a black baby is born to a mother who did not graduate from high school.
- Every 6 minutes a black baby is born at low birth weight, weighing less than five and a half pounds.
- Every 7 minutes a black baby is born to a mother who had late or no prenatal care.
- Every 4 hours a black child is murdered.
- Every 11 minutes a black child is arrested for a violent crime.
- Every 7 seconds of the school day a black student is suspended from public school.

• Every 46 seconds of the school day a black child drops out of school.

The youthful breakdown of morality is a complex issue but the problem is exacerbated when a child is left to his or her devices. Two teenagers in one city were raped repeatedly and then strangled with a belt and shoe laces. The two suspects, also teenagers ranging from 14-18, stomped on the necks of the girls to make sure they were dead. One has to wonder how much time these young criminals had spent being left home alone to think through their plans and then *literally* execute them! In yet another city, three young men executed two teenagers and a 23 year-old by

"The best anti-poverty program for a child is a stable, intact family. The best educational program for a child is a family that values education, takes the child to the library on a regular basis, reads to and *with* the child, thus opening a wide, exciting world of books and knowledge. The best spiritual environment for a child is a family that honors God and His Word and that *takes* — not sends — the child to church and Sunday School, and regards the Ten Commandments as just that: the Ten Commandments and *not* the ten suggestions."

TGB

strangling them and slashing their throats. The two teenagers were children of divorce and their father was on a golfing trip out of the country. They were *home alone.*

Professionals in the field of pediatrics and public health are telling us that we are now seeing aggressive behavior in *early childhood* that once was reserved for late adolescence. But what are we to expect? When families, television, videos, music and *concerts* celebrate sex and violence and display an increasing abuse of women, should we expect anything *but* a reciprocal amount of violent behavior?

The best anti-poverty program for a child is a stable, intact family. The best educational program for a child is a family that values education, takes the child to the library on a regular basis, reads to and *with* the child, thus opening a wide, exciting world of books and knowledge. The best spiritual environment for a child is a family that honors God and His Word and that *takes* — not sends — the child to church and Sunday School, and regards the Ten Commandments as just that: the Ten Commandments and *not* the ten suggestions.

While the clouds are dark on the horizon of America's families I want to remind you, dear reader, that when your love for your child extends to your saying *I will never leave you home alone,* then that will become the first real secure day of the rest of your child's life. When you say "YES, I'll work it out so you don't have to be home alone"... when you say "YES, I'll sit and read with you tonight"... when you say "YES, we'll work a puzzle tonight, pop some popcorn and just spend some special time together"... and when you say NO to music that degrades, and to *peep shows* thinly disguised as *talk shows* that destroy, then you will know that your child is indeed not lost at all.

The Word of God remains tried, tested and true: *Train up a child in the way he should go: and when he is old, he will not depart from it* (Proverbs 22:6).

But children cannot train themselves. That is why they must not be left *home alone*. My friend, do not ever again leave your children *home alone*.

Three Action Steps

1. With God's help, and with the encouragement of my brothers and sisters, I will do my best to make arrangements so my children will never be left home alone.

2. I will teach my children the meaning of NO...and remind them that the word NO is a complete sentence.

3. I will exchange phone numbers with my children's teachers. I will inconvenience myself by going to their school to discuss my children's grades at the end of each grading period. I love my children so much that there is nothing I will not do to support them and see them succeed.

"Now we struggle to find parents who will participate in prayer… parents who will participate in parenting… parents who will participate in providing a secure environment for their children. Momma and Daddy, where are you? Babies are being left home alone enough and the clock is striking 12. *It is midnight — no longer America's finest hour but her final hour.* It is midnight and the clock is running out for our country and our children."

TGB

2

IT'S MIDNIGHT.
WHERE ARE YOUR PARENTS?

𝕴 will call him Marcus, not his real name. For his own protection I will also conceal the city in which he lives. However, Marcus's story is so common in our society today that his story could pass as daily reality for many a black child in any one of our nation's large cities.

Eight year-old Marcus was watching television late one night in a three story walk-up apartment his momma and daddy had rented a few weeks before. There was a bottle of soda in the refrigerator, some peanuts in a dish and a bag of potato chips on top of the television. That was the supper Marcus was to eat that night. No protein, no healthy bone-building food, no well-balanced meal to help this boy's brain grow firm and strong. Worse yet, Marcus was destined to dine alone *again*. It would be the fourth night in a row that a terrified little boy would have to *go it alone* in a tightly compacted world of fear, wondering when

Momma and Daddy would come home before he fell asleep in front of a television program of questionable viewing value for either adult or *child*.

Suddenly, there was a knock on the door. *Who is it?* Marcus cried out. No answer. Terrified, the child ran to his room and hid under the covers. His heart pounding wildly he heard a loud *thud*, then the quickening steps of heavy shoes on the rugless floor. Sobbing into his pillow Marcus feared the worst. The sweat on his brow trickled into his tearful eyes. The sounds of the shoes got closer and closer until he sensed a figure standing over him. What does a defenseless little boy do at a time like this? He cannot run. He cannot hide. He is too small to fight back. Then with his body shaking little Marcus jumped up, threw off the covers...and realized it had all been a terrible dream — a nightmare. He ran to his parent's room for comfort, and that's when his worst fear became reality. His momma and daddy were not there. It was midnight and they had not come home. *Why did they always have to party? Why did they not arrange for someone to take care of him?* The demons of despair had once again captured his soul and disturbed his fragile spirit. He was living the nightmare he thought had ended. Marcus had once again been left *home alone*.

For many years there was a provocative ad on television directed at the delinquency of children in relationship to keeping late hours without their parents knowing where or why. It went... *It's midnight. Do you know where your children are?* Today, that question needs to be reversed to: *It's midnight. Do you know where your parents are?* That is the question Marcus keeps asking night after night. Unfortunately, he is not alone. Parents, where are you? Your children are afraid and they need you to come home.

Momma and Daddy, Where are You?

I wish the story of Marcus were the tale of only one little boy, but I am afraid it is not. It could be repeated a thousand times over

> "Some parents will return to a house ablaze, set afire by little children playing with matches — because they were left *home alone.* Other out-all-night parents will return to children desperately sick from drinking toxic house cleaning products found under the sink — because they were left *home alone.* Others will come home to find their children drunk and sick from getting into the liquor cabinet…or overdosed from getting into their parents' legitimate or illegitimate drug drawer… Still others will live forever with the horrible memories of stretchers being wheeled out the front door with a white sheet over their babies — little children who suffered and died alone… all because they were left *home alone.*"
>
> TGB

night after night in the homes of people of every race, color and creed in these United States. Some parents will return to a house ablaze, set afire by little children playing with matches — because they were left *home alone*. Others will come home to find their children drunk and sick from getting into the liquor cabinet... or overdosed from getting into their parents' legitimate or illegitimate drug drawer. Other out-all-night parents will return to children desperately sick from drinking toxic house cleaning products found under the sink — because they were left home alone. Still others will live forever with the horrible memories of stretchers being wheeled out the front door with a white sheet over their babies — little children who suffered and died alone... all because they were left *home alone*.

So I am compelled once again to ask the question: Momma and Daddy, where are you when you are needed most? What on earth could be more important *at midnight* than your own little Marcus or Sharon or Jamal or Ebony? Surely not a party. Surely not a nightclub. Surely not just *hanging out*. As I write these

---

"It used to be...*it's midnight. Do you know where your children are?* Today, that question needs to be reversed to: *It's midnight. Do you know where your parents are?*"

TGB

---

words the terrible statistics are out: Afrikan American children born today have only a 20% chance of growing in a two-parent family. An even more terrifying statistic is that two-thirds of the first children born to our sisters under the age of 35 are born out of wedlock. These numbers set the stage for what I call the most despicable disappearing act of our time — the "now-you-see them now-you-don't" single parents of our nation's most precious resource: our children. Remember the Whitney Houston theme song?

> *I believe the children are our future. Teach them well and let them lead the way. Show them all the beauty they possess inside. Give them a sense of pride to make it easier. Let the laughter remind us how we used to be...Everybody's searching for a hero. People need someone to look up to. I never found anyone to fulfill that need. A lonely place to be, so I learned to depend on me.*

Sow the Wind; Reap the Whirlwind

Thirty years ago what could have been called *adolescent* irresponsibility today must be re-categorized as *parental* irresponsibility. In just three decades everything has flip-flopped. Now we struggle to find parents who will participate in prayer... parents who will participate in parenting... parents who will participate in providing a secure environment for their children.

Momma and Daddy, where are you? Your babies are being left home alone and the clock is striking 12. *It is midnight — no longer America's finest hour but her final hour.* It is midnight and the clock is running out for our country and our children.

What are the devastating consequences for Afrikan American families that will surely arise from this *national parental disappearing* act? Are they short term or long term? Is it a mere blip on the research screen of a social scientist, or is it a terrible trend that threatens to topple what remains of the black family? In *Boys to Men,* I quoted one of the most knowledgeable communicators on the subject, Haki R. Madhubuti, who in his bold book, *Black Men: Obsolete, Single, Dangerous?* writes...

"The world has gotten worse for black men. A young Black man, according to the U.S. Census Bureau has a one in 21 chance of being murdered as compared to a one in 333 chance for a white man of the same age. One of two black young people live in poverty. The black male prison population is over 50%, whereas our population in this country is around 13%. Of the six leading causes of death among the adult population, black men lead the list in each category: homicide, heart attacks, cancer, suicide, strokes and accidents. The status of blacks is beyond the endangered species category."

This, I submit, is the kind of thing that all too often happens when parents sow the wind: *they reap the whirlwind.* Innocent parental extracurricular activities that keep the children *home alone* build a foundation for future failure. *We do not need to change the constitution, we just need to change our personal situation.* And children cannot do this alone. They need Momma and Daddy to help show them the way. Too many parents say, "I'll do what I want when I want to do it. Let the little ones make it on

> "The world has gotten worse for black men. A young Black man, according to the U.S. Census Bureau has a one in 21 chance of being murdered as compared to a one in 333 chance for a white man of the same age. One of two black young people live in poverty. The black male prison population is over 50%, whereas our population in this country is around 13%. Of the six leading causes of death among the adult population, black men lead the list in each category: homicide, heart attacks, cancer, suicide, strokes and accidents. The status of blacks is beyond the endangered species category."
>
> Haki R. Madhubuti
> *Black Men: Obsolete, Single, Dangerous?*

their own." Fine, if it is your desire to give Madhubuti more sickening statistics for his next book. *Not fine* if you want to help us save our little black brothers, our sisters and our race.

We fail our children when we do not invest in their future, whether by providing them with meaning or money. I've heard too many parents say, "I made mine, now let them make theirs." But the truth is *we all got by with a little help from our friends and family.* The *selfishness* of the age is sabotaging our future. You cannot do enough to provide a firm foundation for your children today. We may make a living by what we get, but brothers and sisters *we make a life by what we give.*

"Sow the wind and reap the whirlwind" is an Old Testament expression of a New Testament reality. The scripture reminds us (Hosea 8:7) that the result of sin and disobedience will always be barrenness and disappointment. Choose life! In Romans 6:23 we find the inescapable: "For the wages of sin is death; but the gift of God is eternal life through Jesus Christ our Lord." Choose life! The theme in the scripture of *sowing the wind and reaping the whirlwind* is an inviolable law of God. While preaching in Australia I learned a great deal about the boomerang, a unique device that is a metaphor for what always happens in real life. Whatever you put out comes back to you, like the boomerang —

> Galatians 6:7 reminds us "Be not deceived;
> God is not mocked: for whatsoever a man
> soweth, that shall he also reap." In the language
> of the street, it means *what goes around comes
> around…or every dirty deal has a two-way ticket.*
>
> TGB

that curved wooden instrument used by Australians for hunting and war. The boomerang is so designed that when thrown a certain way it goes out for many yards, but then makes a huge arc and returns to the hunter. The amazing thing about this ingenious implement is that *you cannot throw a boomerang away.* It just keeps coming back to the place of its origin *because that is how it has been designed.* It is the same way with how you and I live our days: the "boomerang" effect is one of the keys to understanding life.

It is much like the biblical wisdom that says *what you reap you will sow.* Galatians 6:7 reminds us "Be not deceived; God is not mocked: for whatsoever a man soweth, that shall he also reap." In the language of the street, it means *what goes around comes around… or every dirty deal has a two-way ticket.*

It is as solid and reliable as the law of gravity. God's Word

> "God never promised you a rose garden in rearing your children. However, I guarantee if you leave them *home alone,* the weeds will take over the flowers."
>
> TGB

also reminds us in Romans 6:23 that *the wages of sin is death.* The death of which the Scripture speaks comes in a variety of styles and assortments:

- There is the death of marriage.
- There is the death of relationships.
- There is the death of self-esteem.
- There is the death of a child's potential.
- There is the death of hope for the future
- There is the death of love, and yes, even physical death.

Are there any guarantees that your life will be rosy, without problems, complete with effortless sailing to the next port if you *never leave your child home alone?* No, I am afraid there are no guarantees your life will be without its troubles, my brother and sister. God never promised you a rose garden in rearing your children. However, I guarantee if you leave them *home alone,* the weeds will take over the flowers. But before we throw our hands up in despair, we need to remember there are eight more words — encouraging, uplifting, life-changing words — in the last part of

Romans 6:23 to give us great hope in the midst of our predicament. They are... "but the gift of God is eternal life through Jesus Christ our Lord." That is the divine contrast: sin versus grace; death versus life. As the Word of God says in Joshua 24:15, "Choose you this day whom you will ." Praise God we all have a choice. Let us invite those multitudes of little black children who are being left *home alone to come home to Jesus.* Jesus is still the answer for the world today. He is our only hope for this present painful predicament.

Latchkey is *Off* Key

It is documented that most children do not enjoy being left home alone until they approach adulthood. Latchkey children may give all appearances of being tough, cool and even self-reliant, but down deep they are frightened. Many are scared to death. A recent study by the American Academy of Pediatrics studied the subject of substance abuse by some 5,000 eighth-graders in and around Los Angeles and San Diego. The sample cut across racial lines and was evenly balanced between boys and girls of varying economic and ethnic backgrounds. Here are the disturbing results of that study as published in *Current,* September 1991:

> "...12- and 13-year olds who were latchkey kids, taking care of themselves for 11 or more hours a week were about twice as likely as supervised children to smoke, drink alcohol, and use

marijuana. About 31% of the latchkey kids have two or more drinks at a time; only about 17% of the others do. Asked whether they expected to get drunk in the future, 27% of the latchkey kids and 15% of the others said yes."

"...12- and 13-year olds who were latchkey kids, taking care of themselves for 11 or more hours a week, were about twice as likely as supervised children to smoke, drink alcohol, and use marijuana. About 31% of the latchkey kids have two or more drinks at a time; only about 17% of the others do. Asked whether they expected to get drunk in the future, 27% of the latchkey kids and 15% of the others said yes."
American Academy of Pediatrics Report

Many of these latchkey boys and girls are children of mothers who are children themselves. In the August 30, 1993 issue of Newsweek headlined: *A World Without Fathers: The Struggle to Save the Black Family,* we read, "For teenage mothers not mature enough to cope, single parenthood is not the route to the dream, but entrapment. They have too many frustrations: the job, the lack of a job, the absence of a man, the feeling of being dependent on others for help, the urge to go out and dance instead of pacing with a crying child."

Our teenage sisters must be taught the risks of leaving their children home alone. We must help them understand the terror their little ones feel when they are left *home alone* when their only tie to their momma is a house key draped around their necks. It's bad enough today and tomorrow as they come home from school to an empty house, but *an empty home today means an empty life tomorrow.* Jesus tells a horrifying story about what happens in a house where there is no one present. Hear God's Word,

> "When the unclean spirit is gone out of a man, he walketh through dry places, seeking rest; and finding none, he saith, I will return unto my house whence I came out. And when he cometh, he

---

"Too many of our homes are swept clean of love, nourishing, compassion and of parents just *being there* when they are needed. And what happens? The devil and his demons have a field day. They encounter no resistence. Every room is empty and they can move about at will. They occupy that empty home like squatters. They don't pay the rent but they *do* exact payment from the innocent child whose baby-sitter is now Beelzebub.

TGB

---

findeth it swept and garnished. Then goeth he, and taketh to him seven other spirits more wicked than himself; and they enter in, and dwell there: and the last state of that man is worse than the first" (Luke 11:24-26).

What a commentary on contemporary culture. Too many of our homes are swept clean of love, parental guidance and nourishing, compassion and of parents just *being there* when they are needed. And what happens? The devil and his demons have a field day. They encounter no resistence. Every room is empty and they can move about at will. They occupy that empty home like squatters. They don't pay the rent but they *do* exact payment from the innocent child whose baby-sitter is now Beelzebub.

This is all bad enough, but now let us look beyond the immediate problem to the even more questionable future when those children grow up. At this point an even more terrifying scenario comes into view. When latchkey children become teenagers and begin to exhibit those "trying" qualities few of us as parents will *ever* understand anyway, these adolescents, as they defy parental authority, find themselves living with so much stress that the family often completely breaks down because no strong relationship has ever developed between child and parent.

I talked to one latchkey child recently about what it was like to be left *home alone* every day after school. I asked him, "Brother, what's it like to make your own dinner, do your own homework,

> "The keys around the necks of our latchkey children may open the front door of their houses, but they will never open the door to self-esteem. Nor will they open the door to self-respect or to respect for others. They will not open the door to courtesy, to manners, to social skills or academic excellence."
>
> TGB

wash your own dishes and put yourself to bed? There was a long, painful silence. A tear formed in his empty eyes as he threw himself into my arms. His silence spoke volumes.

Latchkey children are scared. They never learn how the world works *because they haven't spent enough time with their parents who are supposed to be there to help them figure it out.* Home is where we learn to make decisions.

Home is where we learn about relationships. Home is where we know there will always be a shoulder to cry on and a lap to sleep on. Home is where a momma and daddy know how to dry tears and help put away a child's fears. But our children cannot do these things alone. Is it any wonder our children are finding so many limits to their success? There are too few parents available to show them the way. The keys around the necks of our latchkey children may open the front door of their houses, but they will

"If you have to choose between saving your child or getting a new coat…

SAVE YOUR CHILD.

If you have to choose between saving your child or getting a new car…

SAVE YOUR CHILD.

If you have to choose between saving your child or going on a trip…

SAVE YOUR CHILD.

If you have to choose between saving your child or buying a new home…

SAVE YOUR CHILD."

TGB

never open the door to self-esteem. Nor will they open the door to self-respect or to respect for others. They will not open the door to courtesy, to manners, to social skills or to academic excellence.

That innocent key that hangs around the neck of our Afrikan American children hangs as a millstone. That key is a burden not a blessing. It weighs a child down instead of picking a child up. When the key goes in the lock to a boy or girl's home he or she wants to say, "Momma, I'm home," but when that boy or girl comes home to an empty house it is the detachment of demons that Jesus talks about in Luke 11 that waits to greet the child with,

> "And he said to them all, If any man will come after me, let him deny himself, and take up his cross daily, and follow me. For whosoever will save his life shall lose it: but whosoever will lose his life for my sake, the same shall save it."
>
> Luke 9:23,24

"Welcome, son, glad to see you. Welcome, daughter, we're happy you're back. Don't worry, we're here with you. You're safe with us, and you're *really* not alone. You have us for company. *Now shut the door and lock it.*" Oh how the demons love it when children are left *home alone.* They jump for joy and shout sadistic satanic slogans when they know they have no one to interfere with their diabolical dialog with a child who has been left *home alone.* So who will it be: the devil or the divine deliverer? The poacher or the priest? The parent or the plunderer?

My brother and sister, we do not have to leave our homes open to the devices of the devil. It simply does not have to be this way. *It must not be this way* because a commitment to our children and a godly personal self-denial can save our children and the race. Let us line up with the truth because the truth never changes. Hear the Word of our God from Luke 9:23-25:

> "And he said to them all, If any man will come
> after me, let him deny himself, and take up his

cross daily, and follow me. For whosoever will save his life shall lose it: but whosoever will lose his life for my sake, the same shall save it. For what is a man advantaged, if he gain the whole world, and lose himself, or be cast away?"

This is a word from the Lord for such times as these...a word from our Omnipotent, Omniscient and Omnipresent God. If we choose not to heed this divine counsel it will be at our own peril and there will be hell to pay.

Remember these words. Mark them in your heart...

"If you have to choose between saving your child or getting a new coat...

SAVE YOUR CHILD.

If you have to choose between saving your child or getting a new car...

SAVE YOUR CHILD.

If you have to choose between saving your child or going on a trip...

SAVE YOUR CHILD.

If you have to choose between saving your child or buying a new home...

SAVE YOUR CHILD."

> "The remote control is the tool for choosing whatever violence a child may want to see.
> It has been said that MTV is our media music teacher. Others have said: MTV — *making tots vicious;* MTV — *making teenagers violent;* MTV — *music to vomit by;* MTV — *mess, trouble and violence;* MTV — *major threat to victory.*"
>
> TGB

Raise Yourself, Little One

When we force a child to stay home alone, we are telling that child to *make it* alone. We are saying, *raise yourself, little one. Come on, you can do it. Yes, you're small and you're not tall, but you can stretch and you can reach. Just keep trying, little one, you can do it by yourself, you don't need your momma or daddy really...you can teach yourself to do all the things that grown-ups do.* Lord have mercy on any and all of us if we say, imply or infer these hostile words in the presence of our children.

When we leave a child home alone we provide the training tools for failure, tools that lie around in great abundance: The remote control is the tool for choosing whatever violence a child may want to see. It has been said that MTV is our media music teacher. Other have said: MTV — *making tots vicious;* MTV — *making teenagers violent;* MTV — *music to vomit by;* MTV — *mess, trouble and violence;* MTV — *major threat to victory.* Is it

> "Your child does not want your things.
> Your child wants YOU. Help us end the cycle
> of confusion and chaos. Help us put
> to rest the *home alone syndrome.*"
> TGB

video soul or video sell out? Is it comedy def jam or comedy *death jam?* The potential for pornography, self-abuse and personal defeat abound in the house of a child who is left *home alone.*

Raise yourself little one. Make your own sandwiches. You choose the clothes you wear. *You* choose the way you do your hair. If you want a friend, the talk show hosts will talk to you. These merchants of the bizarre are ready, willing and able to fill your tender ears with smut unspeakable. *All the best to you little one. Raise yourself, little one. I know you're only 14 and that you're a baby having a baby, but all the best... make it if you can.* And the

> "It is midnight. Where are your parents?
> Are they coming home or will they once again
> leave you *home alone?* Momma and Daddy,
> it is not so much what you say to your child that's
> important; it is what you do that counts...Your
> child does not want things. Your child wants YOU.
> Help us end the cycle of confusion and chaos.
> Help us put to rest the *home alone syndrome.*"
> TGB

beat goes on… *The Home Alone Syndrome.*

It is midnight. Where are your parents? Are they coming home or will they once again leave you *home alone?* Momma and Daddy, it is not so much what you say to your child that's important; it is what you do that counts. It does not matter what you wear, the kind of car you drive, how many designer clothes you have in your closet, or how bountifully your walls are adorned with the artifacts of Africa. Your child does not want things. Your child wants YOU. Help us end the cycle of confusion and chaos. Help us put to rest the *home alone syndrome.*

__Three Action Steps__

1. From this day forward I covenant with my children never — within reason — to leave them home alone. I no longer choose to be part of the problem. From now on my behavior is part of the solution.

2. I will prioritize my work so that my children always come first. If I sow the wind, I know I will reap the whirlwind. With God's help I will succeed in becoming the kind of mother or father God wants me to be. I will make *special arrangements* with my boss to leave early and come in early so I can spend more time at home, so that my child will not be left *home alone.*

3. At this very moment, I am beginning to see myself as a successful parent. Not because of my skills or abilities, but because of my response to God's ability. My child is royalty and deserves to be treated as a child of the King. I will not put it off. Every minute matters. I will do it *now!*

"When your children know they are loved by you and loved by a merciful God, their self-esteem skyrockets; pride in their accomplishments pushes through previous pain; they no longer settle for a life of fear and failure. For this to happen, you have to be a stay-at-home parent. It will not happen if your children are left home alone."

TGB

3

SHORT TERM PAIN...
LONG TERM GAIN

He was the first Afrikan American to play major league
baseball. At the age of six this grandson of a slave was
abandoned by his father, leaving his mother, Mallie,
and the other children to fend for themselves. His mother did
cleaning to support the growing family while the children went to
school and enjoyed a wide range of sports in their free time. They
all did well on the field but there was one boy, Jackie, who was
unusually at home in the tough, unyielding world of competition.
Later, he went on to become UCLA's first four-letter man as he
became the top basketball scorer for two years in a row, won the
national championship in the long jump, and finally was named an
all-American halfback on the gridiron.

After a difficult stint in the U.S. Army, where he was almost court-martialed for refusing to sit in the back of the bus, he returned home to join the Kansas City Monarchs of the old Negro League baseball team. They might have enjoyed the game on the field but once the team left the park it was a different story. Discrimination in hotels and restaurants was rampant and decent compensation for hard work was not even an option. Conditions could not have been worse. Dogs were treated better than the members of the team. But a man named Branch Rickey, the president of the Brooklyn Dodgers, knew talent when he saw it and encouraged Jackie Robinson to leave the Monarchs to join the Dodgers' minor league team, the Montreal Royals. It was a risky move for Branch Rickey but he had already decided it was long overdue to break the color barrier in the national pastime. Rickey was upfront when he told Robinson it would not be easy to be the first black in the league. He promised Jackie he would have to deal with human indignities, discrimination, untold abuse, pressure and racial hatred. He also said he would have to possess virtual superhuman discipline not to let the personal attacks affect his game. They made a deal. Jackie went to the Royals.

Rickey was right. During games outside Canada racial slurs descended on Robinson like so many hailstones in a sudden Midwest storm. As Rickey had predicted Jackie had indeed become the lightning rod for taunts and racial abuse leveled by ignorant, racist fans. The angry words and physical threats finally took their toll as the pressure sent the rising star into a batting slump. To their credit, the Montreal fans continued to come to the park to rally around Robinson and root him on, a support that shook him loose from that slump and led the Royals to the league pennant. Jackie Robinson was on his way.

April 15, 1947. A day which will forever be etched in the hearts of Afrikan Americans — the day Jackie Robinson stepped up to the plate as the first black player in major league baseball. Later, during a game with the Phillies, Robinson endured such a stream of verbal abuse from the opposing dugout that there would have been few men on earth who could have endured the assault. Yet, Jackie Robinson, always the epitome of grace under pressure, let the words of hate bounce off the invisible shield he had built around him and proceeded to play with poise and perseverance. In an instant he won the praise and respect of his teammates along with sportswriters around the country.

Jackie Robinson knew he had to *go through it to get to it.* He knew that he would have to take the slings and arrows of short term pain to enjoy what he knew would one day be *long term gain.* Jackie Robinson, you are no longer with us, but we honor your memory. On October 24, 1972 your great heart for humanity finally could beat no more and you went to your eternal reward. We love you, Jackie, and you will always be in our hearts. So when we complain about our pain, you help us think of long term gain. When our fractured world seems insane, you remind us of

> "When a black man named Simon of Cyrene picked up the cross of Jesus and carried it to Calvary, he became a permanent figure in the hallowed halls of holy history. A black man was the first to pick up the cross and I believe black people will be the last to lay it down. We understand better than most that unearned suffering is redemptive. We know the meaning of the cross, the necessity of the cross and the power of the cross. The cross is "I" crossed out."
>
> TGB

the long term gain. When a national agenda seems inane, from heaven above, we hear you say *brothers and sisters, never give up . . .it's only short term pain for long term gain.*

Jackie Robinson wasn't just a ballplayer. He wasn't even just an Afrikan American who had to buck racism to be able to fulfill his mission in life. Robinson was a pioneer for you and for me. He took the heat alone. He stood up to the racists alone. He didn't have anyone to march for him or with him. He didn't have any other brothers in the dugout. He went to bat, literally, alone — for himself, for you and for me. Everyone of us needs to remember him for that, and to be eternally grateful for the courage he mustered despite all odds. For some I know this may sound like ancient history, but we must never forget the bridges that he brought us over. When we hear the name of the great baseball legend, Jackie Robinson, may we always pause and give a prayer of thanks for this great human being and for what he did for the race.

Jesus said, "In this world ye shall have tribulation, but be of good cheer for I have overcome the world." When a black man named Simon of Cyrene picked up the cross of Jesus and carried it to Calvary, he became a permanent figure in the hallowed halls of holy history. A black man was the first to pick up the cross and I believe black people will be the last to lay it down. We understand better than most that unearned suffering is redemptive. We know the meaning of the cross, the necessity of the cross and the power of the cross. The cross is "I" crossed out. Bob Schuller has said,

> "William O. Walker, the Dean of Black Journalism, knew the pain. His famous words, 'Don't order the coffin yet — the corpse is still ALIVE!' are among the most well-known in the annals of Black History. He knew short term pain would lead to long term gain. Anna Julia Cooper, a tireless crusader for higher education for blacks, knew the pain. She lived from slavery into the civil rights movement. She endured the hurt so we might be where we are today. It was short term pain for long term gain."
>
> TGB

"It is God turning a minus into a plus." The hymn writer penned the words,

> *"Must Jesus bear the cross alone and all the world go free? No, there's a cross for everyone, and there's a cross for me. The consecrated cross I'll bear Till death shall set me free, and then go home my crown to wear, for there's a cross for me."*

Once again, "If any man will come after me let him deny himself, and take up his cross daily and follow me. For whosoever will save his life shall lose it: but whosoever will lose his life for my sake, the same shall find it" (Luke 9:23,24).

Jackie Robinson is not alone. Every brother and sister reading this book knows about the pain. William O. Walker, the Dean of Black Journalism, knew the pain. His famous words, "Don't order the coffin yet — the corpse is still ALIVE!" are among the most well-known in the annals of Black History. He knew short term pain would lead to long term gain. Anna Julia Cooper, a tireless crusader for higher education for blacks, knew the pain. She lived from slavery into the civil rights movement. She endured the hurt so we might be where we are today. It was short term pain for long term gain. Mahalia Jackson left her native New Orleans at age 16 and went to Chicago where she ironed shirts in a laundry, sang in a choir and saved her money to open a beauty parlor. But it would not be shampoo, rinse and curlers for this soldier of the cross. She appeared in Carnegie Hall in 1950 and among her many academic honors was an honorary Doctorate in Humane Letters from Lincoln (Illinois) College. Her legacy was love and lifting up black people through gospel music. She was adored as the world's greatest gospel singer. Mahalia Jackson knew her short term pain would lead to long term gain.

Wimbledon champion Arthur Ashe also knew the pain. A childhood illness left him with only a slight build, but with the able instruction of Ronald Charity, a top-ranked black player, Ashe learned to perfect his strokes. By 1960 he became the American Tennis Association's youngest tennis champion ever. Later, while a student at UCLA, Arthur represented the United States several times as a member of the Davis Cup team. By 1965 he was the top-ranked collegiate tennis player in America and continued to be the driving force for the Davis Cup team. In 1969 he was refused a visa to play tennis in South Africa after which he enlisted the support of various groups to set right this racial wrong. His efforts resulted in the expulsion of South Africa from the Davis Cup competition in 1970. Surely the crowning moment of his meteoric rise in the tennis world was in 1975 when at the age of 31, he beat Jimmy Connors in five sets at Wimbledon. Arthur Ashe had become number one in the world. Many of us, however, will remember this slender giant just as fondly for his moving press conference on April 8, 1992 when he announced to the world that he had contracted AIDS from a blood transfusion following surgery. He, too, paid a price for black people and to him we owe a debt of deep gratitude. Arthur Ashe endured for what he knew would be long term gain.

Shirley Chisholm, one of the most influential black women in America, continues to be a firebrand advocate for human rights. She made history when she campaigned for the democratic nomination for President in 1972, and later wrote in a widely received book titled *The Good Fight* about her valiant bid for that nomination. A specialist in child care and welfare Shirley has known the pain. Like the others in this litany of great men and women she, too, knows it is only short term pain for long term gain.

Basketball great Magic Johnson made some serious mistakes in his quest to be the best on the hardcourts and today knows the pain and the ultimate consequences of being HIV positive. But this superstar never gave up and he never gave in. Today he continues to do something with his life. He is not sitting around moaning his fate. He works through the pain, doing all he can to be of service to others. Any list of memorable Afrikan Americans will invariably leave someone out, but this list cannot even be partially complete without speaking our gratitude to the Pulitzer Prize winning author Alex Haley who gave us *Roots*. Haley labored over his work for twelve years, using the many experiences of his family's background in Gambia and in Tennessee as incentive for his book which became an acclaimed television miniseries. Thank you, Alex. You endured the short term pain to give us all a long term gain.

Why have I begun this chapter with these familiar stories of our Afrikan American brothers and sisters who never let the candle of hope be blown out by external circumstances? For this reason: Every one of us must be willing to take our black babies as seriously, and put as much heart and energy into creating an environment to develop their full potential, as these heroes of the past and present took and take seriously their missions in life. Robinson never gave up. Walker never gave up. Ashe never gave up. Chisholm never gave up. Cooper never gave up. Jackson never gave up. Johnson never gave up. Haley never gave up. And _____ (put your name in that space) is never going to give up either. Starting today, promise yourself and your children you will never quit *regardless of how tough it gets.* Believe in your heart that you will find a way for your family *even when there is no way.* When your child is asked where *home* is may his or her answer always be: *Where Momma and Daddy* are. How your children see the world depends on the world you *show* them. Do not treat your little ones as pit stops on the raceway of life. Take time to be alone *with* them and do not leave them *home alone.* Because when it is all said and done, *a house may be built by hands that are strong, but a home is built by loving hearts.* In its simplest form this is how we sow seeds of greatness into our race. We need a foundation that must be laid in the home where we learn to serve with hearts where love is king and compassion is queen. If we do this, we will *indeed* build a race of Kings and Queens.

Martin Luther King, Jr. reminded us…

> *"Everybody can be great. Because anybody can serve. You don't have to have a college degree to serve. You don't have to make your subject and your verb agree to serve. You don't have to know about Plato and Aristotle to serve. You don't have to know Einstein's theory of relativity to serve. You don't have to know the second theory of thermodynamics in physics to serve. You only need a heart full of grace. A soul generated by love."*

Someone has said, "Service is the rent we pay for the space we occupy." Jesus said in Matthew 23:11 that "…he that is greatest among you shall be your servant."

"The Bible says… *'But without faith it is impossible to please God.'* It also says that *'He that cometh to God must believe that He is, and that He is a rewarder of them that diligently seek Him.'*—Hebrews 11:6 You may not see it all clearly now, but if you persist the payoff will come. Short term pain — long term gain. *You have to go through it to get to it."*

TGB

Five Secrets of Effective Parenting

In *Boys to Men* I said that success comes in cans...*I can, I can, I can, I can.* Your key to detouring demons of despair and destruction is desire. Believe that you *can* make a difference in the life of your child, and then admit that you will never do it alone. As I often say, *once you make up your mind it's just a matter of time.* The Bible says, "But without faith it is impossible to please God." It also reminds us, "He that cometh to God must believe that He is, and that He is a rewarder of them that diligently seek Him" (Hebrews 11:6). *You have to go through it to get to it.* You may not see it all clearly now, but if you persist the payoff will come. Short term pain — *long term gain.* Here are *five secrets* of effective parenting, and special antidotes for the *home alone syndrome.*

1. Create a stable home environment where you can teach your children right from wrong by your daily example of love and discipline. Let these future leaders know that not only did Jesus die to save us but that Jesus lives to keep us. Teach them that Jesus invites us to burden Him with what burdens us. The Master said, "Come unto me, all ye that labour and are heavy laden, and I will give you rest" (Matthew 11:28). When your children know they are loved by you and loved by a merciful God, their self-esteem skyrockets; pride in their accomplishments pushes through previous pain; they no longer settle for a life of fear and failure.

For this to happen you have to be a stay-at-home parent. It will not happen if your children are left home alone.

2. Recognize that parenting is a *joy* not a *job*. Parenting has some tremendous challenges, but it also has some great rewards. We often say in church that "our children, when they are small, they walk on our feet, but when they grow up, they walk on our hearts." That is one of the reasons why parents sometime lose the joy of parenting. They fail to recognize that there is a cross to bear. The words of Maya Angelou speak to the kind of fortitude that is necessary for all of us who assume the awesome role of parenting. She says,

"Courage may be the most important of all virtues, because without it one cannot practice any other virtue with consistency."

For parents, this courage takes five forms:

1. Staying home more and stepping out less.
2. *Working* on the problem instead of *worrying* about it, and realizing that *every problem* is a platform for a miracle.
3. Promising to get better not bitter.
4. Recognizing that when God gives you extraordinary trials he also promises extraordinary triumphs.

> "We often say in church that 'our children,
> when they are small, they walk on our feet,
> but when they grow up, they walk on our hearts.'
> That is one of the reasons why sometimes
> parents lose the joy of parenting. They fail
> to recognize that there is a cross to bear."
>
> TGB

5. Knowing that *attitude* is the only difference
    between success and failure.

3. You Must Go Through It to Get To It. If we are to save this generation of impressionable black children and share with them the joy of living and personal success, we are going to have to suffer with them and suffer for them. This commitment to their safety, security and spiritual destiny starts in the home. There is no easy way — and there is no *other* way. But when parents are consistent then that joy is multiplied in suffering. The scriptures say "To suffer *is* Christ and to die is gain." In the *end, it is short term pain for long term gain.* But you must go through it to get to it. This means words like self-denial, self-abandonment, self-sacrifice, being uncomfortable and inconvenienced must start cropping up in your vocabulary and in your spirit. Again, *it's a cross that you must bear.* Your children did not beg and plead with you to come into this world. If anything, at the time of their birth

> "The Bible says *a child left to himself brings his mother to shame.* Praise God there is a flip side to this tragedy — *but a child not left to himself brings to his mother fame.* She becomes the mother known all over as the mother of that beautiful and blessed child.
>
> TGB

one might interpret their cries as *"I'm not sure I like what I'm getting out of and getting in to!"* Remember, you invited them into this veil of tears. Given our current dilemma it is becoming more apparent in these last days that perhaps we should cry when our babies are born and rejoice when they depart this life. You prepared the way for their noisy entrance. Now it is your God-given responsibility to do what it takes to prepare them for the rest of their lives. Parents, if you expect to wear a parenting crown you must be willing to bear a parenting cross. Let us all get back to the old landmark where parents took their parenting seriously. Why? Because there is victory in those values. There is wisdom in those words…and when we act as if we believe it, we will discover there is *still* a future for our families. What seems like defeat will one day become victory when you believe with certainty that the clouds of evening may be dark and threatening but *joy cometh in the morning.*

Our children are our most significant others. They are our most significant extension. They become our immortality as we discover the joy of parenting is in the journey. The prize is never given to a competitor before the race is run. The fruits of victory are never divided before the battle is won. We must *all* go through it to get to it. It is only through trials and tribulations, testings and tumult that we will ever find ourselves in the winner's circle. The *home alone syndrome* has in it *not* the ingredients that make for joy, but rather the stuff from which discouragement and defeat are born and nurtured. The Bible *says a child left to himself brings his mother to shame.* Praise God there is a flip side to this tragedy — *but a child not left to himself brings to his mother fame.* She then becomes the mother known all over as the mother of that beautiful and blessed child.

4. You Must Bend Your Child Toward God if you want the tree of character, integrity, goodwill and divine purpose to grow

---

"When you *bend your children* toward God you choose to believe the scripture when it admonishes you to *'Train up a child in the way he should go, and when he is old he will not depart from it.' — (Proverbs 22:6)"*

TGB

---

and flourish. Someone was once asked *How tall will a tree grow?* The answer came back, *As tall as it can.* It is the same with our children. Biologically and physically they *will* grow. No question about that. But grow into what? Will they grow into people of character whose lives are shaped in a loving, supportive home where both parents are present? Or, will they develop into misshapen adults of deformed demeanor and compromising character? Parents, the choice is yours, not your children's. When you *bend your children* toward God you choose to believe the scripture when it admonishes you to *Train up a child in the way he should go: and when he is old, he will not depart from it* (Proverbs 22:6). Notice there is no deadline in that verse. It does not say when your boy or girl is 12, or 16, or 25 or 32 that they will not depart from it. But it *does* say *they will not depart from it.* When you believe God's Word and take counsel from the Father who loves your children even more than you do, you move immediately from fear to faith, from hopelessness to hope, from discouragement to delight and from the jitters to joy. But you must *be there* with your child when it counts. You will not enjoy lasting success with your child if you leave your son or daughter *home alone.* Your job is to listen to your child. Your job is to make your dwelling a home not just a house. *Bending your child toward God* means your home will be known as a sanctuary not a sitting room. It will be a familiar family altar not the place for a frequent family feud. Prayer, Bible study, Bible stories, church attendance, a home

> "I cannot legislate morality, but as a parent I can legislate behavior. We need more parents who are 'legislators.' Not with baseball bats, leather straps and cattle prods, but with serious, no-nonsense discipline. *Spare the rod, spoil the child.*"
>
> TGB

free from the toxins of cigarette smoke, an absence of alcohol and other drugs, abusive language and any other abuse — these are the things that create the environment to help you *bend your children toward God.*

There will always be a tension between bending and breaking. Bending a branch — or a child — takes time. You can *break* a branch in an instant. Real parents are aware of the difference. What I call *ego parenting* is when a mother and father are more concerned about themselves than they are about their child.

Discipline with a Capital D

I can still see my grandmother pulling a switch from the tree that stood in front of our home. I can see — oh how I can see it to this day — her stripping off the leaves slowly, methodically, one by one. Once she got that far in the process I knew there would be no retreat. My grandma never retreated. *Spare the rod, spoil the child.* Most of the time she didn't even have to hit me. She just had that *look* in her eyes. My adrenaline would begin to flow as the leaves were pulled from the switch one by one. At that moment, my process of humility went into high gear. With the skills of a drill sergeant, Grandmother would swing the switch in the air giving it a *whistling* sound. *Swish, swish, swish, swish.* She had my attention. Then it came. As the switch found its way to my tender understanding, she would say in rhythm what I had done wrong and what I needed to do about it

In staccato she would say, "Didn't... I... tell... you" (that was four swings worth)..."you... should... not... have... done... that." (six more). "Now... go... up... stairs... and... stay... in... your... room... until... I... tell... you... to... present... yourself... down... stairs." For every word there was a wallop. And with every question from Grandmother I would respond in a kind of antiphony, "Yes... you... did... grand... mother... I'm... real... sor... sorry... real... so... rry."

That is discipline! Parents, we must return to it. However, do your discipline in love, because when done in *anger* it can become *abuse.* But let us stick with the truth of the Bible: *Spare the rod, spoil the child.* I cannot tolerate parents in the supermarket who say to their child, "Now Billy, I've told you 30 times not to touch that. Would you like some candy?" Ridiculous. What kind of message does that send to a child? It is important to address that little brother quickly. He will not die, and he needs to understand before the sweet by and by. You see, you have to give your best to get the best, or as the scripture says, *The measure you give is the measure you get.*

I cannot legislate morality, but as a parent I *can* legislate behavior. That's why we need more parents who are "legislators." Not with baseball bats, leather straps and cattle prods, but with serious, no-nonsense discipline. *Spare the rod, spoil the child.* But when a child is left *home alone* there can be no discipline. When a child is left to his or her own desires, parents are simply saying: *work it out for yourself, little one. Let 911 be your help in time of trouble. Learn your discipline from your heroes on television. Comfort yourself with the fact that 42% of all American kids are left home alone often or at least occasionally. Relax, little one, you are one of 10 million children who are home alone most afternoons almost every weekday. You are among a great number, little one, surely you can figure out how to take care of yourself.*

My brothers and sisters, this is wrong. Dead wrong. We have played with fire too long and we have always gotten burned. Parents, where there is discipline there will be no disappointment. Where there is discipline there will be no disaster. Where there is discipline there will be no defeat. Be there to discipline your child. Do not leave the disciplining to the demons. And do not leave your children *home alone.* An empty house tempts a child to invite in the devourer who arrives in the guise of a friend, but who ends up mauling and maiming innocent children because parents opened a door their little ones were unable to close. **Where there is no discipline disaster abounds.** Before Dr. Benjamin Spock got hold of our parents with his liberalized teaching on child rearing — called "permissive parenting" — most American families knew how to discipline their children. The large majority of boys and girls were disciplined biblically, decisively and physically, if necessary. The *board of education* did not sit downtown; it was held in the hand of a loving mother or father. Discipline gives life, it does not take it. More than once I heard my momma say: "I brought you into this world and I can take you out." I got the message. But a child left *home alone,* without being disciplined in love and compassion, will be a ship without anchor, cast about by every wind of the sea. I am also of the opinion that when they ended the military draft, many of our boys missed the meaning of discipline. It is not a bad idea for someone to *demand* you be responsible. Getting up at 6 a.m., making your bed and bouncing a quarter off of it, shining your shoes each day, saying "Yes, sir," and "No, sir," "Yes, ma'am," and "No, ma'am" all sound pretty good today. But for the past 40 years, we have developed the undisciplined child. Between Dr. Spock and the *age of rock,* the *pill* and an end to the draft, we have seen our children receive the proverbial *shaft.* Our young people are the victims and we are violators. What will the next 40 years bring? *Sow the wind and reap the whirlwind.*

15 Things Real Parents Do

Parents, we need Mom, not Montel. We need Dad, not

Donahue. We need the *child* connection, not the Love Connection. The tragedy is that *All My Children* got caught in a *Secret Storm* on the *Edge of Night* looking for the *Guiding Light* and ended up in *General Hospital.* So what is the lesson in this media madness? If your *Family Feud* leads you to *People's Court* just remember **THAT YOU ASKED FOR IT.** Yes, things have changed. "Coke" used to be a soft drink. "Pot" was once something you put flowers in. "Gay" once meant *happy.* A "closet" used to be something you went *into* and not something you came *out* of. "Crack" was a bat hitting a baseball. My how times have changed, but are we any better *for* the change? I think not. Parents need to quit going the way of the crowd and start going the way of the cross. We must give up to go up. There is *no express elevator to the top* when it comes to child raising. We all have to walk the stairs one step at a time. That means parents have to start staying home, staying honest and staying humble before the Lord.

"Satan is not after our material, he is after our minds. He is not after our cars, he is after our children. He is not after our finances, he is after our families. And the surest way he will win the day is for parents to slide down the slippery slope of Sodom and leave their children home alone."

TGB

- Parents must have principles that are constant.
- Parents must have priorities that never change.
- Parents must preach possibilities and promise.
- Parents must ponder the power of persistence.
- Parents must put the rod to work where necessary.

Parents, wake up! Save your child and you save an adult. Save an adult and you save a family. Save a family and you save a church. Save a church and you save a community. Save a community and you save a city, a nation and the world. *But it all starts with saving the child in YOUR HOME and by refusing to leave your little one home alone.* In *Boys to Men* I wrote of *Twenty-Five Things Real Men Do.* Those 25 suggestions have become so helpful and popular that I have been asked by hundreds of readers to create a set of *must do's* for parents. Here is my list of *Fifteen Things Real Parents Do:*

1. Real parents discipline their children in a disciplined way. Real parents don't break up, they make up.
2. Real parents don't spoil the child and spare the rod.
3. Real parents know the best teaching is by example *caught* not *taught.*
4. Real parents are both tough-minded and tenderhearted.
5. Real parents recognize that a spanking in love is simply short term pain for long term gain.

6. Real parents *take* instead of send their children to church. Real parents do not *prey* on their children, they *pray* for them.

7. Real parents turn off the TV at supper time because they realize if they don't turn *off* the news their children will wind up *in* the news.

8. Real parents do not play around, they stay around.

9. Real parents do not rely on the lottery, they rely on the Lord.

10. Real parents do not divorce, they are devoted.

11. Real parents love their children and know that God has a unique plan for their lives.

12. Real parents train them in the play pen so they won't end up in the state pen.

13. Real parents discipline them in the high chair so they won't end up in the electric chair.

14. Real parents know that if they take their children to the prayer chamber they will avoid the gas chamber.

15. Real parents provide their children with prayer and not pistols; they don't give them guns, they give them God.

As I close this chapter, I do so thinking about you who are parents and grandparents. You do not have it easy. Not one of us, including myself, can measure up to the *Fifteen Things Real Parents Do.* But you and I, through the power of Almighty God, had better try. The devil is loose and roams our neighborhoods and our "living rooms" as a roaring lion seeking whom he may devour. But Satan is not after our material, he is after our minds. He is not after our cars, he is after our children. He is not after our finances, he is after our families. And the surest way he will win the day is for parents to slide down the slippery slope of Sodom and leave their children *home alone.* That is not what real parents do. Let us no longer permit the media, with its methodical and maniacal manipulation of our minds, to make a mockery of our men, women, boys and girls. Enough with dirty soaps, lewd lyrics, raunchy rap, violent videos, comedy *death* jam and video violence. Is it really funny that virtually every black comedian has a major part of his act as a cross dresser or female impersonator? Here we go again...fathers abandoning mothers...mothers loving boys, boys imitating their mothers...going from their mothers' laps to their wives' laps without ever growing up (or as I said in *Boys to*

Before Dr. Benjamin Spock got hold of our parents with his liberalized teaching on child rearing — called "permissive parenting" — most American families knew how to discipline their children. The large majority of boys and girls were disciplined biblically, decisively and physically, if necessary. The *board of education* did not sit downtown; it was held in the hand of a loving mother or father. Discipline gives life, it does not take it.

Men, "...or without ever making the transition.")

Take control, parents. If you do not assume the reins of leadership with your children, the pimp will, the prostitute will, the drug man will and the devil will. It will not be easy to stand your ground in the midst of so great a temptation, but with God at your side you will soon discover that any amount of short term pain is well worth the long term gain. That is ultimate joy. That is victory. That is living life as God meant it to be lived. It all starts when you realize once and for all that a house is not a home — the subject of Chapter Four. *Jesus is in the house!*

Three Action Steps

1. I know that the best parenting is when by example truth is *caught* and not necessarily *taught.* I am taking control of the environment of my home and making it a kingdom for my child. And I will *not* leave my child *home alone.*

2. I realize that without discipline there can be no real love. I know that without a godly discipline there can only be disaster. I am learning to discipline my child and I know in my heart it is worth *the short term pain to enjoy the long term gain.*

3. I believe the words of Martin Luther King, Jr. who said that if we are to live the life of a servant we need *a heart full of grace.* I commit before God to becoming a loving, kind, responsible parent. I recognize my awesome responsibility as a mother or father to be God's person in the presence of my child. I will not wait to become this kind of person. I am becoming that person *now!*

"God's Word reminds us that 'And ye shall know the truth and the truth, shall make you free.' — (John 8:32) As we seek that truth in Christ we soon realize it is impossible to know 'all the answers' without knowing Him Who is the answer. Our social scars will remain if we do not know Him. Our political problems will persist if we do not know Him...and the home alone syndrome will continue to kill our children and ruin our families unless we acknowledge our need of a Saviour."

TGB

*"Isn't it a shame? A black man invented the clock
and we still have black folks who don't know what time it is."*
Jewel McCabe

4

A HOUSE IS NOT A HOME

hile walking down a street in the historic section of Petersburg, Virginia recently, I came across a sign in front of a huge house that read: *The House of Folly.* Intrigued by the sign, I inquired why such a large, beautiful dwelling with so many luxurious rooms had been designated as *The House of Folly.* After a brief inquiry I received my answer. I learned that the builder and former owner of post Civil War mansion had kept the workers laboring for many years, only to end up with a large house in which he would live all alone. No sounds of childish laughter would ever echo throughout the lavishly designed halls. No homework would be done in front of the fireplace on those cold Virginia nights. No first dates would come to the door to take his daughters out for the evening. No prayers would be said at the bedside of a son who might be struggling in his quest to become a man. Instead, the *House of Folly* was little more than a monument to one man's ego. It was a shrine to selfishness; a garish gesture of greed. The owner's life's motto was not *give me liberty,* it was simply *give me.* He was wrapped up in himself and was overdressed. Like the legions of the living death that inhabit our communities and churches, he was "all dressed up with no place to go." He had created a mausoleum of memories dedicated to money and had filled his empty rooms with equally empty objects that would not satisfy. Yes, the man had built a big house, but it was not a blessed home. It was the *House of Folly.*

Today in this country we have many houses that are houses of folly — not because there are *no* children living there, but because there is no one there to make it a *home* for the children. We have become a *nation of folly.* We are a nation *of* children but we have little concern *for* our children. We birth our children but we do not bless them. We pay the rent but we don't pay attention. We turn on the gas but we turn off God. Parents, it may have walls, windows and winding staircase and wall coverings, but without love and laughter it is only a house, and a house is not a home. Wall-to-wall drapes and a freezer full of steaks don't make a home if in that house there is nothing but wall-to-wall confusion and communication is frozen.

You have to be at home to make it a home, and it will be *no home* if you leave your little ones *home alone.* I have said it earlier and I will say it again, and again, and again: *If there is no parenting cross, there will be no parenting crown.* In the long run the cross you *take up* will always be easier than the one you *throw down.*

> "We birth our children but we do not bless them. We pay the rent but we don't pay attention. We turn on the gas but we turn off God. Parents, it may have walls, windows and winding staircase and wall coverings, but without love and laughter it is only a house, and a house is not a home. Wall-to-wall drapes and a freezer full of steaks don't make a home if in that house there is nothing but wall-to-wall confusion and communication is frozen."
>
> TGB

Heaven in Your Home

I have discovered that we can have heaven in our churches and heaven in our homes. If someone wanted to see how they are worshipping in heaven, all we need do is stop by your church. If someone wanted to see how they are living in heaven, they only need to stop by your house. You want heaven on earth? I will tell you where you must search first: *in your own home.* If people want to know what heaven is like, *invite them into your home.* If they want to know how children are treated in heaven, *invite them into your home.* If they want to see how husbands treat wives and wives treat husbands in heaven, *invite them into your home.* What is heaven like? "Come on over for supper and see for yourself." This is heaven on earth. But it doesn't happen in a house; it

> "If we do not *believe* "Thy Kingdom come,
> thy will be done on earth as it is in heaven,"
> we ought to stop praying the prayer."
>
> TGB

> "Give me one hundred men
> Who love nobody but God,
> Who hate nobody but the devil,
> Who read no book but the Bible,
> And I will shake hell's foundation
> And establish the Kingdom of Heaven On Earth."
>
> John Wesley

happens only in a home. If we do not *believe* "Thy Kingdom come, thy will be done on earth as it is in heaven," we ought to stop praying the prayer.

Five Ways to Make Your House a Home

A house is not a home unless it provides sustenance for the soul as well as bread for the body. What has happened to the family altar? What has happened to make the television our teacher and the tape machine our tutor? In the past the family broke bread together; today that same family itself is broken, split apart, with parents *doing their own thing* and leaving their children *home alone.* I want to give you five important ways to help you make your house a home…

1. Fear the Lord Your God and Love Him with All Your Heart and communicate your faith *faithfully* to your children. Families who fear God can face life fearlessly; families who do not fear God wind up fearing everything — *and they communicate that fear to their children.*

- The Bible says "The fear of the Lord is the beginning of knowledge..." (Proverbs 1:7).
- Psalm 111:10 teaches us that "The fear of the Lord is the beginning of wisdom..."
- Psalm 34:11 says, "Come, ye children, hearken unto me: I will teach you the fear of the Lord."
- In Psalm 147:11 the psalmist writes, "The Lord taketh pleasure in them that fear him, in those that hope in his mercy."
- Proverbs 10:27 reminds us, "The fear of the Lord prolongeth days: but the years of the wicked shall be shortened."

My what a prophetic verse for 21st century families in America. Are not the days of our children being shortened? Is not the *home alone syndrome* signing the death warrant to our best and brightest? In my hometown of Indianapolis, of the 766 cases referred to juvenile court in one recent month, only 16 percent involved children from families that had both mother and father at home. The majority came from single-parent households. Parents, the math is simple. *When there is only one parent at home, the ability to supervise a child is cut in half.* When only one parent is at home, the ability to teach a child *moral values* is cut in half. When only one parent lives at home, the opportunity *to influence a child for good* is cut in half. When only one parent lives at home, the privilege of teaching a *child to fear God and love Him with all his heart* is cut in half. *It's just that simple.* Our local newspaper recently quoted a superintendent of the detention center who said that many of the kids keep coming back to the facility *to get the nurturing and caring they are not getting anywhere else.* What an indictment on parents who leave their children *home alone.* One probation report after another shows how mothers and fathers are too busy to be bothered by their children. My brother and sister, *that is sin.* That is "sowing the wind and reaping the whirlwind." The pattern will continue UNLESS...our homes learn to fear God and love Him with all our heart. As I said in *Boys to Men,* it takes a man to teach a boy how to be a man; conversely, it takes a woman to teach a girl how to be a woman.

2. Make God's Word Your Guiding Light in everything your family thinks, does and says. Horace Greely once said "It is impossible to mentally or socially enslave a Bible-reading people." But the American family in general — along with too

> "Parents, the math is simple. *When there is only one parent at home, the ability to supervise a child is cut in half.* When only one parent is at home, the ability to teach a child *moral values* is cut in half. When only one parent lives at home, the opportunity to *influence a child for good* is cut in half."
>
> TGB

> "Horace Greely once said 'It is impossible to mentally or socially enslave a Bible-reading people.' But the American family in general — along with too many of our black families — are enslaved, and this time we cannot blame it all on white racism alone, although the legacy can never be discounted. The fact of the matter is that without God's Word read in our homes we enslave ourselves."
>
> TGB

many of our black families — *are* enslaved, and this time we cannot blame it all on white racism alone, although the legacy can never be discounted. The fact of the matter is that without God's Word read in our homes we enslave ourselves. If we fail to do our spiritual duty as parents, we will soon discover that a child left to his own devices will turn to the book of pornography before he will turn to the book of Psalms. A child left *home alone* will turn to promises of the demons before she turns to the poetry of David. Once again, John Wesley wrote, "I want to know but one thing — the way to heaven... God himself has condescended to teach the way. He hath written it down in a book. Oh, give me that Book. Here is knowledge enough for me. Let me be a man of one Book." One of the concepts that attracted me to the Christian Church (Disciples of Christ) was their emphasis on The Book. They espoused "no book but the Bible and no creed but Christ. Where the scriptures speak, we speak, and where the scriptures are silent, we are silent." Denominations have demons, too. The Christian Church (Disciples of Christ) like many other mainline denominations have strayed from the mark, lost the Book, and as a result are suffering great consequences. *Lord, make our Afrikan American fathers, mothers and children people of the Book, not just members of a church. Help us all to know that we CAN live by bread alone providing it is the BREAD OF LIFE.*

A poet has written...

> Despite the cynic's angry word,
> The skeptic's narrow look
> The running ages have not matched
> The holy, mighty Book.

Parents, if you want to turn your house into a home, make God's Word *a lamp unto your feet and a light unto your path.* It is not just a way to happiness and hope for the survival of your family, it is the *only way.*

3. Teach your Children the Joy of Working. The Bible reminds us that *One who does not work should not eat.* Unfortunately, some parents despise work. They regard their J-O-B as meaning *just...over...broke* and they communicate those negative thoughts about work to their children. Well, that just won't cut it any more. Remember most of the attitudes learned in the home are caught not taught. *You've got to go through it to get to it.* There is no substitute for hardwork. The welfare system in this country has been instrumental in taking away our incentive for labor and has helped make us entertainers instead of entrepreneurs. It's been said that in a storm you can pray to God all you want, but you had better row for shore. Variety may be the spice of life, but it is the *monotony of labor* that "brings home the bacon." If you will read between the lines throughout God's Word you'll notice that we seldom hear much about the resolutions of the redeemed, but we hear a great deal about the Acts of the Apostles. The poet certainly told it like it is as he penned these lines...

> Although it may seem
> That the process is slow,
> Still, work is the yeast
> That raises the dough.

Someone has said, "Pray as if everything depended on God (and it does) and work as if everything depends on you (and it doesn't). Proverbs 10:16 reminds us, "The labour of the righteous tendeth to life: the fruit of the wicked to sin." If you want to make

> "It's been said that in a storm you can pray to God all you want, but you had better row for shore. Variety may be the spice of life, but it is the *monotony of labor* that 'brings home the bacon'."
>
> TGB

your house a home, teach your children — by example and spirit — *the joy of working.*

4. Live Within Your Means. Pat Warren, senior editor of *Urban Family,* suggests 7 WAYS TO EASE FINANCIAL STRAIN in the Winter 1994 issue of that magazine. Her titles are worth repeating. My comments are in parentheses.

1. Disconnect the cable. (You don't need to watch most of the movies anyway. They will just pervert your mind and poison your children.)
2. Use credit cards only under strict guidelines. (If you can't pay the full amount on your credit card bill at the end of the month, *don't use your credit card.* If you only use greenbacks you'll have no set backs.)
3. Reconsider holiday shopping. (Make things for your children at Christmas. Borrow a dress to wear at a wedding. Rent a tux. Do not buy

emotionally just because it is that *season of the year.*)

4. Avoid the "sales" trap. (Do not get "hooked" by sale items. This merchandise is probably not even worth the discounted price. It is all too easy to go broke saving money.)

5. Eat out less. (Instead of *fried fast food* try *friendly family food* for a change. Make your time around the breakfast and supper table interesting for your children. Ask questions about school, their grades and their goals.)

6. Be an organized grocery shopper. (Plan your meals for a week or more in advance. Avoid impulse buying. Buy good, healthy food. Too many stops at the *convenience* store can put you in a situation where you have too much month left after the money runs out.)

7. Shop till you drop — NOT! (Do not use *shopping* as therapy for curing the blues. Find other ways to get happy that will be more productive and less costly. Take your child to the zoo, to the library, to a church function — or just spend some time with your child with no schedule at all. Just *be there* with your son or daughter. It could well be the most important day in your child's life.)

5. Teach your Children an Attitude of Gratitude. If you pause to *think* about Him, you'll have cause to *thank* Him. Think about how God has blessed you with your children and let your sons and daughters know how much you thank God for them. Don't make gratitude an occasional incident; make it a continuous attitude. If *you* are not thankful for what you have, your children will never be thankful for what *they* get. The Bible is filled with verses that admonish us to be thankful:

> "*Giving thanks* always for all things unto God and the Father in the name of our Lord Jesus Christ (Ephesians 5:20).
>
> "Rooted and built up in him, and stablished in the faith, as ye have been taught, abounding therein with *thanksgiving*" (Colossians 2:7).
>
> "Be careful for nothing; but in every thing by prayer and supplication *with thanksgiving* let your requests be made known unto God" (Philippians 4:6).
>
> "I will praise the name of God with a song, and will magnify him with *thanksgiving*" (Psalm 69:30).

One of the most beautiful expressions of how a child's sense of self-esteem is nurtured and developed is portrayed in the following prose piece by an unknown author. Mark these words, parents, and let their practical power be a constant challenge to you to remember it is *by your example* that your children learn

> "My grandmother could cut me to the quick when she would say, 'You, my son, are an ingrate.' Too often, she was right about my actions though wrong about my motives."
>
> TGB

both the good and the bad...

IF A CHILD...

If a child lives with criticism, he learns to condemn.

If a child lives with hostility, she learns to fight.

If a child lives with ridicule, he learns to be shy.

If a child lives with shame, she learns to feel guilty.

If a child lives with tolerance, he learns to be patient.

If a child lives with encouragement, she learns confidence.

If a child lives with praise, he learns to appreciate.

If a child lives with fairness, she learns justice.

If a child lives with security, he learns to have faith.

If a child lives with approval, she learns to like herself.

If a child lives with acceptance and friendship, he learns to find love in the world.

Parents, the first *real* day of your child's spiritual and emotional growth starts when *by example* you teach your sons and daughters an attitude of gratitude. *But you must go through it to get to it.* It takes time to make a lasting impression, so you must be consistent. The longest journey begins with a single step in the right direction. Your children will not and cannot learn to give thanks if they must do it on their own... and they will be hard pressed to realize their God-given potential if they are left *home alone.*

The Secret of Your Power

During my many weeks of research prior to writing *The Home Alone Syndrome,* I discovered page upon page of how thinkers worldwide have perceived and defined power. Here is a sampling of some of the wisdom of the ages...

- Nearly all people can stand adversity, but if you want to test somone's character, give him power.
- There is nothing in the world more powerful than an idea. No weapon can destroy it; no power can conquer it, except the power of another idea.
- Knowledge is power only when it is turned on.
- Power will either burn a man out or light him up.
- The greatest power for good is the power of example.
- There is more power in the open hand than in the clenched fist.
- A person with compassion wields more power than someone with muscle.
- Prayer provides power, poise, peace and purpose.

This will be a better world when the power of
love replaces the *love of power.*

Where do you get *your* potential for power? How do you
define power for yourself? What is the *secret* of your power? How
do you use your power to make your house a home? Hopefully,
you have already taken to heart the many practical examples of
how to exercise your God-given power given in this book. But let
us look yet further at this subject by searching the scriptures for
the *real* secret of a parent's power. Hear the Word of the Lord…

- "The Lord is slow to anger, and great in *power,*
  and will not at all acquit the wicked…" (Nahum
  1:3).
- "But if thou wilt go, do it, be strong for the
  battle… for God hath *power* to help, and to cast
  down" (II Chronicles 25:8).
- "For the kingdom of God is not in word, but in
  power" (I Corinthians 4:20).
- "For I am not ashamed of the gospel of Christ:
  for it is the *power* of God unto salvation to every
  one that believeth…"(Romans 1:16)

Brothers and sisters, do you have eyes to see and ears to hear
what the Word of God is saying to you as parents? The power is
turned on when you are not ashamed of sharing the Saviour. The
power is turned on when you see the secular as subject to the

sacred. The power is turned on when you realize your every problem is a platform for a miracle. The power is turned on when you realize only the truly great are humble — and only the humble are truly great. The word of Truth reminds us: *Humble thyself and let God exalt thee.* Again, we read in Luke 9:23 and 24,

> "And he said to them all, If any man will come after me, let him deny himself, and take up his cross daily, and follow me. For whosoever will save his life shall lose it: but whosoever will lose his life for my sake, the same shall save it."

This is the true secret to your power.

But...you will give away your power if you do not use it to train your children in the way that they should go. You *lose* your power if you gain the whole world and forsake your own child. That's why God wants you to *use* your power to discipline, delight in and develop your child into the person the Master wants him or her to be. But you cannot accomplish this if you leave your children *home alone.* Your power will vanish like a vapor if you live for self and turn your sons over to Satan. Parents, do not forget or forsake your children. Do not leave it to them to figure out their future. Do not leave them *home alone* in tenantless, unoccupied, abandoned, deserted and desolate homes. *Sow the wind, reap the whirlwind.* Do not leave your children *home alone* with a free bar, VCR tainted tapes that you have stashed, compromising checks that you have cashed and messy magazines that you have trashed. The *Home Alone Syndrome* is killing us. We have already traded bullet proof vests for the whole armour of God. We have traded hats with slogans for helmets of *salvation*. I predict if we stay on the road to ruin that by the turn of the century it will be standard issue for families to wear bulletproof vests to church. Bulletproof windows in our automobiles will be as common as air bags. But you can help change that dismal view of the future *today* because *you are the power. Jesus lives in you, and Jesus lives in your house.* That means you mothers and fathers will have to take *less* so your children may have *more.* It is not an option. It is the answer to the *home alone syndrome.* It is God's way of helping you to make your house a home.

"The power is turned on when you are not ashamed of sharing the Saviour. The power is turned on when you see the secular as subject to the sacred. The power is turned on when you realize your every problem is a platform for a miracle.."

TGB

"It does not do you any good to sit up and take notice if you just keep sitting."

TGB

It Takes a Whole Village to Raise a Child

It is up to us as Afrikan Americans to glean the best from our royal heritage in our eternal effort to raise our children to be the men and women God created them to be. That is why the Afrikan proverb "It takes a whole village to raise a child" is so vital to our children's spiritual, social and emotional growth. This timeless saying captures the essence of the healthy development of our young brothers and sisters. It implies a community that cares about *all* our children. It speaks of a society that shares its resources with every child who needs them. It means there are brothers and sisters who dare to speak up and speak out when a child — any child — is slipping off the edge. When a *whole village raises a child,* support for that boy or girl comes from everyone. In this setting the infant is lovingly led into childhood; the child is gently guided into early adolescence; the young adolescent valiantly ventures beyond the home and into a friendly community where he or she learns the ways of adulthood; the older adolescent increasingly develops self-confidence that *he is right with the world* as he now assumes the task of helping to train another young brother or sister. May God help us believe — and put into practice — this wisdom from our Afrikan ancestors… *It takes a whole village to raise a child.* I will always be grateful to Mr. and Mrs. Frank Jones Sr. who lived on my street and had permission to stay on my "case." They were a part of that extended village that both disciplined and developed me.

"The Afrikan proverb 'It takes a whole village
to raise a child' is so vital to our children's spiritual,
social and emotional growth. This timeless saying
captures the essence of the healthy development
of our young brothers and sisters. It implies a
community that cares about all our children. It speaks
of a society that shares its resources with every child
who needs them. It means there are brothers and
sisters who dare to speak up and speak out when
a child — any child — is slipping off the edge."

TGB

"When it comes to *brotherhood,*
it seems nowadays that there are too
few brothers and too many hoods."

TGB

Martin Luther King, Jr. was right: "What affects me
directly affects all indirectly. I can never be what I
ought to be until you are what you ought to be.
This is the interrelated structure of reality. Either we
live together as brothers or we perish as fools."

Martin Luther King, Jr.

Let us reclaim both the brotherhood *and* the neighborhood. It is time we get back to the next door neighbor knowing all about little Jamal — and having the permission to deal with that little brother if he gets out of line. *It takes a whole village to raise a child.* It is time we realize that when God writes *opportunity* on one side of the door, he writes *responsibility on the other.* We must be a community that cares about our children — your children, my children, their children. It does not do you any good to sit up and take notice if you just keep sitting. *It takes a whole village to raise a child.* Here is a story of a 15 year-old girl whom I will call Tamika. The "village" didn't care enough about this young sister to touch her or reach out to her. The result of that inaction is written in her own painful words. . .

"After two years of sex education and everything mamma told me, I figured I could write the book about sex and boys. The only think I didn't learn was how to tell mamma I was pregnant. And how do I get Steven back? Mom'll be so angry she'll kill me. All she wants me to do is to get out of high school and go to junior college. She's been saving money every since I was five years old. That's when daddy left.

I can hear her now, 'Why weren't you in school? Why weren't you doing your homework? Didn't you have enough chores? Didn't I tell you not to open the liquor cabinet or smoke my cigarettes? I thought you were at the mall. When did you have time for your boy friend?' That one's easy. I had lots of time.

School's a drag. I do all right, but I'm no genius. Besides, we get out early lots of times. After school, I used to go to Steve's house because his folks were never there.

At first we just watched TV and felt each other out, but that turned into sex before I even thought about saying no. You can't go back to just holding hands after all that. I thought we were having fun. Not babies.

Steve used to love me, I think, but now he doesn't even know my name. He's ashamed of me. I thought if I kept the baby I'd at least have something to call my own. I'd like to talk it over with mama, but she's not home half the time. I hate being home alone. How am I gonna tell her? She always told me about the pill. Now forget the *pill*. I'll be buying Pampers.

I don't even know what a diaper looks like. Sometimes I'm happy, and then sometimes I'm so scared I feel like killing myself. But I'm not that brave. I'm really scared. I'm gonna be old and I'm not even 16 yet.

How will I finish school? At least I'll have the baby and he — or she — will love me, even though Steve doesn't. I'll love my baby forever. I'll be OK. Really, I'll be OK. Won't I? Mamma, please tell me I'll be OK. Mamma, are you listening? Mamma, turn the TV down and get off the phone and listen to me... I'm going to have a baby, mamma!"

Parents, Tamika was left *home alone* — one of millions of our precious children who is more *left* than she is lost. In Tamika's case the "village" didn't step in to help. No one tried to help Tamika stay away from alcohol, cigarettes, and sex. No one saw her failing in her studies. No "Mrs. Jones" next door stepped in or stopped by to give Tamika a helping hand, a hug or even a "hello." No one saw the symptoms in time, or else they just turned away because they had other more pressing things to do. The loneliest place on earth is a heart where love is absent.

There is Hope

But thank God there is hope. Lord knows we are aware of the problem of children in our "village" who are being left *home alone.* Here at Light of the World, God is doing a *new thing.* We made a conscious decision to establish a *Village of Hope* in our community right in the midst of the mess. The dope slangers, the gang bangers, the street corner hangers are all a part of the village. Instead of jumping all *over* them, we need to bring Jesus *to* them. They will not come to us, so we must go to them. The church must stop fishing in its own aquarium and move out into the deep. Jesus continues to say to the believer, *Launch out into the deep and use the bait the fish like. Don't change the gospel, but change its*

"Adults are history; children are destiny."

TGB

"We made a conscious decision to establish a *Village of Hope* in our community right in the midst of the mess. The dope slangers, the gang bangers, the street corner hangers are all a part of the village. Instead of jumping all *over* them we need to bring *Jesus to* them. They will not come to us, so we must go to them. The church must stop fishing in its own aquarium and move out into the deep. Jesus continues to say to the believer, *Launch out into the deep and use the bait the fish like. Don't change the gospel, but change its package so it is right down to the modern time.* Our churches are too inflexible and insecure. Holiness is a life-style, not a dress style. We can be so heavenly minded that we are no earthly good. As my younger brothers and sisters say: "Do you comprehend what I recommend?"

TGB

package so it is right down to the modern time. Our churches are too inflexible and insecure. Holiness is a life-style, not a dress style. We can be so heavenly minded that we are no earthly good. As my younger brothers and sisters say: "Do you comprehend what I recommend?"

The *Village of Hope* houses our *Respect Academy* that

interested thousands of you after you read about it in *Boys to Men*. We will soon be expanding our facilities and will dedicate the nation's first *Respect Academy*. We have already suspended our national television outreach in order to address the #1 priority of our ministry: Children, our future. *Adults are history; children are destiny.*

Now a merciful God has blessed us with a community of bold black families who are beginning to see the light. We are starting to light candles rather than curse the darkness. We are choosing to become involved with our little brothers and sisters. We are finally on the look out for the lost and will not let up until we locate those who are *left.* We are totally committed, with God's help, to using all the resources of the "village" to help raise our children. This is the one key solution to the *home alone syndrome.* Are you ready to join forces with the "village" in your area to help save our babies and save our race? Brother, are you willing to be a male mentor to black boys who have no father? Will you stand by them in their studies, be there at their ball games, participate in their pain and be jubilant when they are joyful? Sister, will you take the time to help save a child like Tamika from personal pain? Will you inconvenience yourself to watch out for girls who are being left *home alone?* It is my prayer that you will join our growing "village" of responsive and responsible representatives of God's redeeming power and help us do what we can to take what are only *houses* and help turn them into *homes.* With God's help, and the joyful joining together of brothers and sisters everywhere, we *shall overcome.* We have done it before, and we will do it now. May the *home alone syndrome* become a thing of the past because God's people — one of whom is holding this book in his or her hands — said YES to a child who has been left *home alone.*

Three Action Steps

1. Before God, I refuse to allow my child to be left *home alone.* I will make my house a home, and I will talk with my child, read to my child, instruct my child, and pray with my child. I will never again allow the demons of despair to demonstrate their demonic power within the walls of my home.

2. I covenant with the Father today that the Bible will be the ONE BOOK above all other books and magazines in my home. I will read the scriptures daily to my child, and I will show my son or daughter *by my example* what is right.

3. From today forward, *gratitude* will not be an occasional incident, but rather a continuous *attitude* in my home. I will always be thankful for what I have so my children will be grateful for what they get. I will praise the name of God with a song in my heart and I will magnify His name with *thanksgiving.* But I cannot do it if I am not at home. I do not want to be part of the *home alone syndrome.* I promise to be a stay-at-home parent. Never again will I leave my precious child *home alone.*

*It's hard to hold an AK-47 in one hand
and Isaiah 47 in the other.*

TGB

* * *

*I have only just a minute,
Only sixty seconds in it,
Forced upon me—can't refuse it,
Didn't seek it, didn't choose it.
But it's up to me to use it.
I must suffer if I lose it.
Give account if I abuse it,
Just a tiny little minute—
But eternity is in it.*

Benjamin Mays

POSTSCRIPT

A Closing Word..."Jesus Is the Answer!"

amily life in America is at an all time low. Our children are in trouble. Children are killing children for the first time in our history. In Brooklyn, New York, grade schoolers are wearing bulletproof vests. In Washington, D.C., 11 year olds are planning their funerals instead of their birthday parties. Who do we blame—the children or the parent? Aren't the children the victims? Let's stop blaming the children and start blessing them by not leaving them *home alone.* It is true for both the home and the school, that:

When parents came out, the perpetrator came in
When prayer came out, pistols came in
When values came out, violence came in
When authority came out, anarchy came in
When discipline came out, the devil came in
When morals came out, mess came in.

"What can wash away our sins? Nothing but the blood of Jesus. What can make us clean within? Nothing but the blood of Jesus."

Yes, Jesus is the answer! The Bible is the Book. And, the Church is the place. Parents are going to have to rediscover holiness in order to restore happiness in the home. Jesus, firmly fixed in the life of a child, is the best hope for the future. Our parents and children need a personal relationship with Christ. A focus on faith in Jesus Christ will revive the family and family life in America. Jesus is the answer! We have tried everything else, why not Jesus? Get to know Jesus as a family by studying the Bible together daily so that Jesus can speak to you. *It's hard to hold an AK-47 in one hand and Isaiah 47 in the other.* Do not neglect speaking to Jesus through the power of prayer. There is something to the old cliché that "a family that prays together stays together". Don't forget that the church is still the place of values and victory. Parents, you cannot expect a child to go where you won't go. Our nation and our families need to come back to the church, back to the Bible, and back to prayer because it is as true today as it was millennia ago in 2 Chronicles 7:14:

"If my people, which are called by my name, shall humble themselves, and pray, and seek my face, and turn from their wicked ways; then will I hear from heaven, and will forgive their sin, and will heal their land. "

Why don't you give it a try in your home today and everyday? God will save our children. But, don't we have to do something?

Jesus is still the answer. The Bible is still the Book. And, the Church is still the place!

A Closing Prayer...

ou have now completed reading The Home Alone Syndrome. It has been filled with stories, statistics, ideas, thoughts and feelings. It has also provided solutions to one of the greatest tragedies of our time — the millions of children who *daily* are left *home alone*. It is my hope as you have moved through these pages that you have recognized that the best laid plans of the ablest of men and women are not enough for success in this venture. *We need a Saviour to help us see our way through* — NOW! Jesus is still the answer. The problem is that time is not on our side; time is on God's side. The late, great educator, motivator and President of Morehouse College in Atlanta, GA. Dr. Benjamin Elijah Mays, wrote an immortal piece of free verse poetry that reminds us...

I have only just a minute,
Only sixty seconds in it,
Forced upon me—can't refuse it,
Didn't seek it, didn't choose it.
But it's up to me to use it.
I must suffer if I lose it.
Give account if I abuse it,
Just a tiny little minute—
But eternity is in it.

We must win back self-respect, our families and our communities. We must rise from our slumber and become activists. However, we can do nothing in our own strength alone: Our boat is too small and the ocean is too wide. But with our hand in the Master's hand we can — and will — be part of a miracle. If you have never met this Master face-to-face, I encourage you to do it now by simply saying "Lord Jesus, I invite you into my life. Fill me with your Holy Spirit and make me whole." If Jesus is already your Saviour and Lord this may be the hour for you to decide to come back to the Father after years of wandering away from His tender care. He stands waiting, eager to welcome you home. Regardless of where you stand in relation to Jesus Christ, I want to bring this book to a close by praying for you and whatever challenges you may be facing at this time in your life...

Father, may each reader of this book receive Your Sovereign Protection. You have promised all of us that You would never leave us or forsake us. We have a written guarantee that You remain the same yesterday, today and forever. You want us to slow down, follow Your precepts, and renew our strength through *Your* strength. You want us to mount up with wings as eagles, to run and not be weary, to walk and not faint. You also want the millions of little children who are being left *home alone* right now to know You and Your power. You are mightier than the enemy of our children, and we trust You to give us the wisdom and insight to tackle the *home alone syndrome* in the power of Almighty God.

Father, at this moment we lift up before You our black families who struggle to make ends meet. Give them the patience and the perseverance to carry on. We pray that many *villages of hope* will rise up across this nation and throughout the world (we have already had inquiries from London) and make a difference in the lives of our precious children. We pray with the psalmist: *Create in me a clean heart, O God, and renew a right spirit within me.* Dear Lord, I ask You to use this book to help sensitize and stimulate us all to be Your men and women at this time of crisis. We believe in miracles, and we really need a miracle right now. We love You and are grateful that You are our Father. Because "when our mother and our father forsake us, the Lord will take us up." In the Precious Name of Jesus, I pray, Amen.

TGB

Bonus Study Guide
Chapter One
The Home Alone *Sin*drome

Introduction:
Family life in America has changed. Parents suffer from *role confusion* and children are seldom taught godly discipline and responsibility. Parents need their children and children need their mothers and fathers. The African proverb is true: *A single bracelet does not jingle.* If we are to make any significant progress in bringing spiritual health to our homes, parents must *not* leave their children *home alone.*

Key Thoughts:
- AIDS is destroying our children in record numbers, and is the greatest killer of young adult males between the ages of 25 and 44.
- The discipline of our children is vital. Proverbs 29:15 says, "The rod and reproof give wisdom: but a child left to himself bringeth his mother to shame."
- A black child is the product of the black woman and black man who must deal with the pressure and pain of bigotry and white racism on a daily basis.
- We must learn from the wildebeest. This Afrikan animal *stays with the pack, stays on track, never looks back, and keeps on running.*

Vocabulary: Write out the meaning of each term:
- Societal neglect
- Television "peep shows"
- The "Me Decade"
- Parental Delinquency

Questions to Discuss:
1. What is the one major thing you learned from this chapter?
2. Why is this a *left* not a *lost* generation? Be specific.

Bonus Study Guide
Chapter Two
It's Midnight. *Where are Your Parents?*

Introduction:
There was once a television reminder that said, *It's midnight. Do you know where your children are?* Today, it is becoming necessary to reverse the order of that statement. The story of Marcus is one of millions of American children who have been left *home alone.*

Key Thoughts:
- The *boomerang* keeps coming back to its place of origin because that is how it has been designed. This *boomerang effect* is one of the keys to understanding life.
- God never promised you a rose garden in rearing your children. However, if you leave them alone, it's an absolute guarantee that the weeds will take over the flowers.
- Latchkey children may pretend they are tough, cool and self-reliant, but down deep they are scared to death.
- Children don't want *things.* They want their parents to *be there* to talk to them, read to them, play with them and love them. No little child wants to be left *home alone.*

Vocabulary: Write out the meaning of each term:
- Toxic
- Sabotage
- Whirlwind
- Parental Delinquency

Questions to Discuss:
1. What are the two major things you learned from this chapter?
2. What does Dr. Benjamin mean when he quotes Hosea 8:7, which reads, *Sow the wind and reap the whirlwind?*
3. What does Dr. Benjamin mean when he reminds us *You have to go through it to get to it?* Give two examples from your own life.

Bonus Study Guide
Chapter Three
Short Term Pain...Long Term Gain

Introduction:
   This chapter talks about the many Black Americans who had to *tough it out* to fulfill their missions in life: Jackie Robinson, Mahalia Jackson, Magic Johnson, Julia Cooper, Arthur Ashe, and others. Dr. Benjamin reminds us that parents must take their children as seriously as these great men and women took their goals in life seriously. This chapter encourages parents *never to quit regardless of how tough it gets. Keep looking for a way even when there is no way.*

Key Thoughts:
   - The important thing is to recognize what you do not know — and then *learn it.*
   - A black man was the first to pick up the cross of Jesus, and black people may be the last to lay the cross down.
   - A house may be built by hands that are strong, but a home is built by loving hearts.
   - Dr. King taught, "Everybody can be great, because anybody can serve. You only need a heart full of grace. A soul generated by love."

Vocabulary: Write out the meaning of each term:
   - Discrimination
   - Color barrier
   - Short term pain...Long term gain
   - Ego parenting

Questions to Discuss:
1. What are the two major things you learned from this chapter?
2. What did you glean from the Jackie Robinson story? Can you relate to his struggle?
3. What does Dr. Benjamin mean when he says, "Success comes in CANS?" Give three examples.

Bonus Study Guide
Chapter Four
A House is Not a Home

Introduction:

Dr. Benjamin reminds us that "We birth our children but we do not bless them. We pay the rent but we don't pay attention. We turn on the gas but we turn off God." Some parents think that because their children have a roof over their heads that is all that is needed. But it takes much more than that to make a house a home.

Key Thoughts:

- Families who fear God can face life fearlessly; families who do not fear God end up fearing everything.
- It is impossible to mentally or socially enslave a Bible-reading people. Without God's Word in our hearts we are enslaving ourselves.
- Variety may be the spice of life, but it is the *monotony of labor* that "brings home the bacon."
- If you pause to think about God, you will have cause to *thank* God.

Vocabulary: Write out the meaning of each term:

- A nation of folly
- Impulse buying
- Supplication
- Whole Armour of God

Questions to Discuss:

1. What are the two major things you learned from this chapter? Explain.
2. Is your house a *home?* How do you know if it is or is not? Give examples.
3. What did you feel as you read the story of Tamika? Do you think her story is an isolated example? Why? Why not?

PARTIAL BIBLIOGRAPHY
OF "MUST" READING

Benjamin, Jr., T. Garrott, <u>Boys to Men.</u> Indianapolis: Heaven on Earth Publishing House, 1993.

Comer, James P. and Alvin F. Poussaint, M.D., <u>Raising Black Children,</u> New York: Plume, 1992.

Hendricks, Howard G., <u>Heaven Help the Home.</u> Wheaton: Victor Books, 1990.

Kimbro, Dennis, <u>Daily Motivations for African-American Success.</u> New York: Ballantine Books, 1993.

Kunjufu, Jawanza, <u>Developing Positive Self-Image and Discipline in Black Children.</u> Chicago: African American Images, 1984.

Madhubuti, Haki, <u>Black Men: Obsolete, Single, Dangerous?</u> Chicago: Third World Press, 1990.

Morgan, Patricia, <u>The Battle for the Seed,</u> Tulsa: Vancom Inc., 1991.

Smalley, Gary and Trent, John, <u>The Hidden Value of a Man.</u> Colorado Springs: Focus on the Family Publishing, 1992.

Dotson, Dr. James and Gary L. Bauer, <u>Children at Risk.</u> Dallas: Word Publishing, 1990.

Dotson, Dr. James, <u>Parenting Isn't For Cowards.</u> Dallas: Word Publishing, 1987.

For further information on how to order Dr. Benjamin's books, posters, ministry items and messages on video and audio cassettes through our catalog, or to participate financially in this vital ministry through Dr. Benjamin's weekly television, tapes and sermons, please call:

1-800-543-2836

Heaven on Earth Publishing House

P.O. Box 18088

Indianapolis, Indiana 46218-0088

(317) 547-2273

Office of Administration

* * *

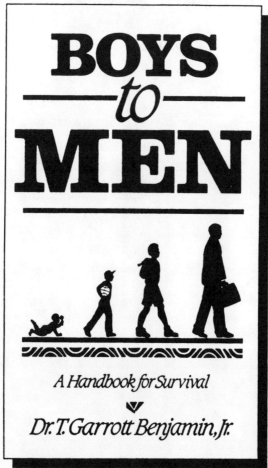

CALL NOW TO ORDER
this best-selling poster
from Dr. Benjamin's book
"Boys To Men"
10 Things Real Men Do

10 Things Real Men Do

1. Real men put away toys and pick up tools.

2. Real men do not just play - they pray.

3. Real men do not just party - they participate.

4. Real men do not just hang out - they work.

5. Real men do not just date - they develop.

6. Real men who are single and saved, know there is no such thing as safe sex - only saved sex. Any sex without the benefit and blessing of marriage is hazardous to physical and spiritual existence.

7. Real men do not just father a baby - they become a father to the baby.

8. Real men do not just love them and leave them - but they love them and help them... bless them and hold them, support them and take care of them.

9. Real men take care of their babies... pay their support, and pay it on time, in the right amount, with some extra thrown in.

10. Real men respect and cherish women as Daughters of the Nile...as descendents of Eve, an African woman who is the Mother of all civilization. (This makes racism even more ridiculous, because Black or White, we have the same mother!)

DR. T. GARROTT BENJAMIN JR.

1-800-543-2836

TO ORDER ADDITIONAL COPIES OF...

The Home Alone Syndrome: A Parent's Handbook for Survival **$12.00**
Home Alone Audio **$5.95** Home Alone Video **$14.95**
Boys to Men: A Handbook for Survival **$10.00**
Boys To Men Audio **$5.95** Boys To Men Video **$14.95**
Boys To Men Study Guide **$1.00**
Boys To Men Poster **$5.00**
Home Alone Poster **$5.00**

When ordering The Home Alone Syndrome, The Boys To Men book and The Boys To Men Study Guide, the total cost for the two books and one guide is $17.00.

	Price	Quantity
Home Alone Book	_____	_____
Home Alone Audio	_____	_____
Home Alone Video	_____	_____
Boys To Men Book	_____	_____
Boys To Men Audio	_____	_____
Boys To Men Video	_____	_____
Boys To Men Study Guide	_____	_____
Boys To Men Poster	_____	_____
Home Alone Poster	_____	_____
Total Ordered	$ _____	
Handling/Mailing	$1.00	
TOTAL PRICE	_____	

METHOD OF PAYMENT:

____Check
____Visa # _____Exp. Date_____
____MasterCard # _____Exp. Date_____
Signature _____
Name_____
Mailing Address _____
City_____ State _____ Zip _____
Telephone _____

Return order form along with check or money order payable to:

Heaven on Earth Publishing House
P.O. Box 18088
Indianapolis, Indiana 46218-0088
(317) 547-2273

Telephone orders may be placed to 1-800-543-2836
Please allow 4-6 weeks for delivery

NOTES

NOTES

_____

_____

_____

_____

_____

_____

_____

_____

_____

_____

_____

_____

_____

_____

_____

_____

_____

_____

_____

_____

_____

_____

_____

_____

NOTES

NOTES